SRA
BUILDING
Vocabulary
Skills

Level 5
Student Edition

McGraw Hill SRA

Columbus, Ohio

SRAonline.com

Printed in the United States of America.

Send all inquiries to:
SRA/McGraw-Hill
4400 Easton Commons
Columbus, OH 43219-6188

ISBN: 978-0-07-623556-8
MHID: 0-07-623556-4

1 2 3 4 5 6 7 8 9 QWD 16 15 14 13 12 11 10 09

Table of Contents

Unit 5

Unit 6

Vocabulary List

1. **foe**
   (fō) *n.*
   enemy

2. **dominate**
   (dom´ ə nāt´) *v.*
   to control

3. **calculate**
   (kal´ kyə lāt´) *v.*
   to figure out

4. **strenuous**
   (stren´ ū əs) *adj.*
   requiring great effort

5. **cunning**
   (kun´ ing) *adj.*
   clever

6. **underdog**
   (un´ dər dôg) *n.*
   the one expected to lose

7. **elimination**
   (i lim´ ə nā´ shən) *n.*
   removal

8. **conspiracy**
   (kən spir´ ə sē) *n.*
   secret, illegal plan

9. **aggression**
   (ə gresh´ ən) *n.*
   hostile attack

10. **pursue**
    (pər sōō´) *v.*
    to strive to accomplish; to chase

"Competition" Vocabulary

1 Word Meanings

Contrasting Words

 Underline the word that signals a contrast in each sentence below. Then circle the word or words that mean the opposite of the boldfaced vocabulary word.

1. In the American Revolutionary War, many people expected England to be the winner, whereas America was thought to be the **underdog.**

2. The British wanted the addition of new taxes, but the American colonists called for the **elimination** of these high taxes.

3. When the American colonists protested the taxes, British troops responded with acts of **aggression** rather than attempts to ensure peace.

4. The British thought that the Boston Tea Party was a **conspiracy;** however, the colonists considered it a fair and open plan for protecting their rights.

5. The colonists had once thought of England as their friend, but now England was their **foe.**

6. Instead of being foolish, the Spanish governor of Louisiana was **cunning** and came up with a plan for secretly helping the colonists.

7. Both sides in a war have to **calculate** rather than guess which strategies the opponent will use.

8. Although the English wanted to **dominate** Florida, they had to give up control when the Spanish forced them to abandon their forts.

9. Surviving the winter was **strenuous** for Washington's soldiers at Valley Forge instead of being easy to bear.

10. The American colonists chose not to give up but to **pursue** independence—and they won.

2 Reference Skills

Guide Words

 Write the vocabulary word that fits between each pair of guide words below.

1. fodder/folk _____

2. dollar/dominion _____

3. caiman/calendar _____

4. straw/streptococcus _____

5. cultured/cure _____

6. undependable/underling _____

7. eligibility/emaciate _____

8. conspicuous/construe _____

9. agency/agonize _____

10. Purple Heart/pusillanimous _____

• •

Draw a line from each word below to its meaning.

11. elimination	**A.** requiring hard work
12. cunning	**B.** angry assault
13. strenuous	**C.** taking out
14. underdog	**D.** the one not favored
15. foe	**E.** smart and quick-thinking
16. aggression	**F.** agreement to act illegally
17. conspiracy	**G.** opponent
18. calculate	**H.** to rule by power
19. dominate	**I.** to follow
20. pursue	**J.** to determine mathematically

Vocabulary List

1. foe
2. dominate
3. calculate
4. strenuous
5. cunning
6. underdog
7. elimination
8. conspiracy
9. aggression
10. pursue

 3 Build New Vocabulary

Context Clues

Read the paragraph below. Then use context clues to answer the questions about the boldfaced words.

The Great War

Great Britain and the United States of America were **allies** during World War I (1914–1918). These former foes joined with several countries to **vanquish** the German forces who conspired to dominate Europe. The number of lives the British lost in the war was **unprecedented** in their history—never before had so many of their soldiers died in battle. Known in Great Britain as the "Great War," World War I was famous for **trench** warfare, a kind of defense that involved fighting in deep ditches. Four years of strenuous **combat** ended with the German army's collapse and the signing of a cease-fire agreement on November 11, 1918.

1. Based on the paragraph, *allies* means _____.
   A. groups joined together
   B. foes fighting each other
   C. countries

2. Circle the word that means the same as *vanquish*.
   A. move
   B. celebrate
   C. conquer

3. Based on the paragraph, *unprecedented* means _____.
   A. occurring often
   B. not completed
   C. not happening before

4. Reread the paragraph and write the definition of *trench*.

   _____

5. Based on the paragraph, *combat* means _____.
   A. fighting
   B. hitting a ball
   C. talking

 **Word Play**

Analogies

 Complete each analogy below with the correct vocabulary word. Use a dictionary if you need help.

> Analogies show relationships between words.
>
> An antonym analogy is *tall is to short as up is to down.*
>
> A synonym analogy is *tiny is to miniature as gigantic is to huge.*

1. **Friend** is to **companion** as **rival** is to

_____ .

2. **Harmony** is to **peace** as **attack** is to

_____ .

3. **Winner** is to **loser** as **favorite** is to

_____ .

4. **Easy** is to **hard** as **effortless** is to _____ .

5. **Keeping** is to **saving** as **erasing** is to

_____ .

6. **Draw** is to **illustrate** as **chase** is to

_____ .

7. **Shake** is to **tremble** as **plot** is to _____ .

8. **Kind** is to **cruel** as **unwise** is to _____ .

• •

Earn two points by writing an analogy of your own. Use either synonyms or antonyms in your analogy.

_____

_____

1. **coordinate**
   (kō or' də nāt') *v.*
   to arrange or place in
   correct order

2. **alliance**
   (ə li' əns) *n.*
   an agreement to
   join together

3. **voluntary**
   (vol' ən ter' ē) *adj.*
   done by choice

4. **accommodate**
   (ə kom' ə dāt') *v.*
   to have or make room
   for; hold

5. **tolerate**
   (tol' ə rāt') *v.*
   to accept or allow; to
   endure

6. **comply**
   (kəm plī') *v.*
   to agree to follow

7. **acknowledge**
   (ak nol' ij) *v.*
   to admit to be true

8. **compromise**
   (kom' prə mīz') *v.*
   to settle difference by
   giving up something

9. **comrade**
   (kom' rad) *n.*
   close friend

10. **enlist**
    (en list') *v.*
    to join a group
    or cause

"Cooperation" Vocabulary

 **1** Word Meanings

Comparing Words

 Underline the word or words in each sentence that signal a comparison. Then circle the word or phrase that defines the boldfaced vocabulary word.

1. Like their **alliance** in World War II, the United States, Great Britain, and the former Soviet Union made an agreement to create the United Nations.

2. By forming the UN, these three countries **acknowledged** that there must never again be a world war; many other countries also admitted the same.

3. Millions of American men **enlisted** to fight in World War II; similarly, many American women joined the war effort by working in factories.

4. Just as the UN brings countries together as friends, it helps individual people become **comrades.**

5. When the UN was formed in 1945, 51 countries agreed to **comply** with its rules, and today more than 180 countries agree to follow the rules.

6. The UN headquarters in New York City **accommodates** thousands of people; the office in Switzerland also has space for many people.

7. The UN does not **tolerate** actions that could lead to war; in the same way, it does not accept the unjust treatment of people.

8. A country's decision to join the UN is **voluntary,** just as its decision to leave the international organization is optional.

9. In the same way that the Security Council of the UN arranges peace efforts, the Children's Fund **coordinates** doctors and other workers to provide help for children around the world.

10. Leaders of nations must often **compromise** to solve political disagreements, like children who must be willing to give up something to settle an argument.

2 Reference Skills

Dictionary Entries

 Read the following dictionary entry. Then match each part of the dictionary entry to its name.

> **accommodate** (ə kom′ ə dāt′) *v.,* **ac • com • mo • dat • ing**
> **1.** to hold; to have or make room for: *The inn can accommodate 20 guests.* **2.** to help; to do a favor or service for; oblige.

1. (ə kom′ ə dāt′)

2. *The inn can accommodate 20 guests.*

3. ac • com • mo • dat • ing

4. to hold; to have or make room for

5. *v.*

6. to help; to do a favor or service for; oblige

A. part of speech

B. second definition

C. additional form

D. phonetic spelling

E. first definition

F. example sentence

• •

 Write the number of the definition of *accommodate* used in each sentence.

7. The new refrigerator can accommodate three 15-pound turkeys. ☐

8. When we asked for a new fork, the waiter was happy to accommodate us. ☐

9. In the Middle Ages, peasants were expected to accommodate the lord of the manor's wishes. ☐

10. The Titanic, a famous luxury cruise liner that sunk in 1912, was built to accommodate more than 2,000 passengers. ☐

Vocabulary List

1. coordinate

2. alliance

3. voluntary

4. accommodate

5. tolerate

6. comply

7. acknowledge

8. compromise

9. comrade

10. enlist

 3 **Build New Vocabulary**

The Prefixes *co-* and *com-*

Add the prefixes *co-* and *com-* to the words below to form new words. Then use the box below to write the definition of each new word.

Prefix	New Word	Definition
1. *co* + exist =	_____	_____
2. *co* + operate =	_____	_____
3. *co* + sign =	_____	_____
4. *com* + pact =	_____	_____
5. *com* + bat =	_____	_____

Definitions

armed fighting with enemy forces

to sign a document with another person

to live together

to work together for a common purpose

packed together; arranged in a small space

 **Word Play**

Yes or No Questions

 Write *Yes* or *No* to answer the questions below.

1. Are most houses large enough to accommodate an airplane?

    _____

2. Could your comrades be your mom and dad?

    _____

3. Could you coordinate a double date?

    _____

4. Does a good citizen comply with the law?

    _____

5. If membership in a club is voluntary, does that mean that the

    members are forced to join? _____

6. Does it make sense to form an alliance with a comrade?

    _____

7. Would wearing a bathing suit help you tolerate cold

    weather? _____

8. Are you creating conflict if you compromise?

    _____

9. Can a person enlist in the U.S. army?

    _____

10. Do most people acknowledge that the world is round?

    _____

1. **publicly**
(pub′ li klē) *adv.*
in a manner open
to all

2. **propaganda**
(prop′ ə gan′ də) *n.*
beliefs spread to
gain supporters

3. **ballot**
(bal′ ət) *n.*
a secret, written vote

4. **advocate**
(ad′ və kit) *n.*
person who openly
supports a person
or cause

5. **politician**
(pol′ i tish′ ən) *n.*
person elected to
office

6. **polls**
(pōlz) *n.*
place where votes
are cast

7. **suffrage**
(suf′ rij) *n.*
right to vote

8. **allegiance**
(ə lē′ jəns) *n.*
loyalty to a country
or ruler

9. **delegation**
(del′ i gā′ shən) *n.*
group of
representatives

10. **swear**
(swâr) *v.*
to make a solemn
promise

Vocabulary for Politics

① Word Meanings

Brainstorming

 Read the following brainstorming concepts. Choose the vocabulary word that each concept describes and write it in the blank.

1. Something done out in the open so everyone can see

   _____

2. Place where you can decide who will be president

   _____

3. Group of people who represent other people

   _____

4. Someone who wants everyone to know they think pollution is

   wrong _____

5. What you use to vote _____

6. Supporting your country _____

7. Being allowed to say who you want to be president

   _____

8. Saying that you will do something no matter what

   _____

9. The president is an example of this

   _____

10. It convinces others to agree _____

② Reference Skills

Syllabication

 Divide each vocabulary word below into syllables using dashes.

1. publicly _____

2. propaganda _____

3. ballot _____

4. advocate _____

• •

Circle the corresponding word parts used to correctly divide the vocabulary words at the end of the lines.

5. The right to vote in elections is called *s-, suf-, suffra-uffrage, frage, ge.*

6. A person who is involved in the government is a *poli-, polit-, po-tician, ician, litician.*

7. To declare something openly is to declare it *publ-, public-, p-icily, ly, ublicy.*

8. Beliefs spread to convince people are called *propag, pro-, propa-, anda, paganda, ganda.*

9. A ticket that is secretly cast to vote on someone is a *bal-, ba-, ball-lot, llot, ot.*

10. To make a serious and sincere promise is to *sw-, swe-, swear. ear, ar.*

• •

 Think About It

Remember that words can be divided between any syllables, except when it would leave one letter alone on a line. One-syllable words are not divided. Which two vocabulary words in Lesson 3 would never be divided at the end of a line?

Vocabulary List

1. publicly
2. propaganda
3. ballot
4. advocate
5. politician
6. polls
7. suffrage
8. allegiance
9. delegation
10. swear

3 Build New Vocabulary

The Latin Root *voc*

 The following words all come from the Latin root *voc*, which means "to call" or "name." Match each word below to its correct definition and write the letter of the definition in the blank. You may use a dictionary if you need it.

A. a sound produced through the human mouth

B. a letter of the alphabet that represents a sound produced with the mouth open

C. a list of words

D. a singer

E. readily expressing one's views through speech

F. to cancel or call back

1. revoke (Hint: *re-* means "to take back") _____

2. vocabulary   _____

3. vocal   _____

4. vocalist   _____

5. voice   _____

6. vowel   _____

• •

 Use the words from above to complete these sentences.

Victor plays the violin with Veronica the

_____. She can vibrate her

_____ on the _____

letters—that is called *vibrato.* Victor's violin does not speak with

_____ but with a variety of pitches and

varying volume.

Word Play

Tongue Twisters

Use the vocabulary words to complete the following tongue twisters. (**Hint:** Some words are used more than once.)

1. Paula the _____ publicly produced

   _____ at the polls.

2. Ali is an active _____ of America's

   _____ with all allies.

3. The seven sisters _____ to

   support women's _____ .

4. The blank _____ belong by the
   blue box.

5. Denver's _____ delayed declaring a
   decision.

6. Patrick _____ promoted his sister
   Patrice for president at the parade.

7. Many people arrived at the _____ to
   pick the next politician for their party.

8. The pamphlets that people push to promote their opinions are

   forms of _____ .

9. Before our secret society sessions we

   _____ to always stay strong and sincere.

10. We predicted before going to the _____

    who the next _____ was to be
    appointed.

Vocabulary List

1. **provoke**
   (prə vōk′) v.
   to make angry

2. **compliment**
   (kom′ plə mənt) n.
   spoken praise

3. **intention**
   (in ten′ shən) n.
   purpose

4. **propose**
   (prə pōz′) v.
   to suggest or put
   forward

5. **plead**
   (plēd) v.
   to beg

6. **viewpoint**
   (vū′ point′) n.
   way of thinking

7. **prohibit**
   (prō hib′ it) v.
   to forbid by authority

8. **brainwash**
   (brān′ wôsh′) v.
   to persuade a person
   completely to change
   his or her beliefs

9. **yield**
   (yēld) v.
   to give way or give
   up; to submit

10. **inspiration**
    (in′spə rā′ shən) n.
    a good influence

Persuasion Vocabulary

1 — Word Meanings

Which Word?

 Circle the vocabulary word that best completes each
sentence below.

1. Dr. Martin Luther King, Jr.'s *(compliment/intention)* was to
   achieve equality and freedom for all African Americans.

2. Because many African Americans shared King's
   (viewpoint/plead), he became their leader and spokesman.

3. King did not want his speeches to *(propose/provoke)* his
   supporters into acting violently.

4. In the 1960s, some states in the South *(prohibited/yielded)*
   African Americans from sitting in certain seats on public buses.

5. Rosa Parks, an *(intention/inspiration)* to those who supported
   civil rights, is famous for refusing to sit in the back of the bus.

6. Parks would not *(provoke/yield)* to the driver's demands that
   she allow a white passenger to have her seat.

7. Rather than *(brainwashing/ pleading)* to be treated with
   respect, Parks expected to have equal rights.

8. Both King's and Parks' actions led the government to
   (plead/propose) new laws to ensure equal rights for African
   Americans.

9. The Nobel Peace Prize, which King received in 1964, was not
   only an honor but also a *(compliment/intention)*.

10. King fought against those who would *(brainwash/yield)* others
    into believing that all people are not created equal.

② Reference Skills

Using a Thesaurus

For each set of words below, cross out the word that is *not* a synonym of the boldfaced vocabulary word. Use a thesaurus to check your answers.

1. praise · ballot · **compliment** · congratulation

2. tolerate · ban · forbid · **prohibit**

3. **plead** · argue · appeal · dominate

4. **intention** · elimination · purpose · goal

5. enrage · **provoke** · block · vex

6. foe · influence · **inspiration** · impulse

7. **viewpoint** · position · opinion · height

8. surrender · submit · **yield** · enter

9. suggest · challenge · **propose** · present

10. **brainwash** · sway · anger · convince

• •

Write the letter of the word that is an antonym for each boldfaced vocabulary word below.

| **A.** calmed | **B.** allowed | **C.** discouragement | **D.** resist |

11. Mahatma Gandhi was an **inspiration** to Dr. Martin Luther King, Jr. _____

12. Like Gandhi, King would not **yield** ground in his fight to spread peace and equality. _____

13. Even when his speeches **provoked** his opponents, King continued to declare his principles. _____

14. Violence during any of King's speeches was **prohibited.**

_____

Vocabulary List

1. *provoke*

2. *compliment*

3. *intention*

4. *propose*

5. *plead*

6. *viewpoint*

7. *prohibit*

8. *brainwash*

9. *yield*

10. *inspiration*

3 Build New Vocabulary

The Prefix *pro-*

The prefix *pro-* is from Latin. It means "forward" or "bringing forth."

 Choose the correct definition from the box for each word below. Write the letter of the correct definition in the blank. You may use a dictionary if you need help.

1. procession _____

2. protrude _____

3. prospect _____

4. produce _____

5. progress _____

6. provoke _____

7. propose _____

8. promote _____

A. a group of persons moving forward in a line

B. forward movement toward a goal

C. a thought of something that one looks forward to

D. to raise in rank or position

E. to put forward for others to consider

F. to bring forth anger

G. to stick out

H. to bring forth; to create

 **Word Play**

Revising Sentences

 Replace each underlined word or group of words with a vocabulary word that is more specific.

1. Thank you for the <u>nice thing you said about me</u>!

   _____

2. Lewis Carroll's <u>thinking</u> on writing stories was that they should

   entertain adults and children alike. _____

3. Koko the gorilla's <u>deeply felt goal</u> was never to harm the kitten

   she dearly loved. _____

4. If you want the school to install vending machines, why not <u>bring forward</u> the idea at the next school board meeting?

   _____

5. In the book, *Cat, You Better Come Home*, by Garrison Keillor, the cat <u>complains and begs</u> constantly to be allowed outside.

   _____

6. When King Midas thinks that gold is dearer than human life, has he been <u>led to believe in something that he wouldn't</u>

   <u>normally believe in</u>? _____

7. That yellow street sign means "<u>move out of the way</u>."

   _____

8. Peggy Fleming has been <u>a role model and person to look up to</u>

   for young ice skaters since the 1960s. _____

9. Taking pictures at a live music concert is usually <u>not allowed</u>.

   _____

10. It was wise for Jack not to <u>annoy, tease, and anger</u> the giant at

    the top of the beanstalk. _____

Vocabulary List

1. **utter**
(ut´ er) *v.*
to state

2. **summon**
(sum´ ən) *v.*
to send for

3. **commend**
(kə mend´) *v.*
to praise

4. **insult**
(in´ sult) *n.*
a rude remark

5. **announce**
(ə nouns´) *v.*
to make known
publicly

6. **murmur**
(mûr´ mər) *v.*
to speak in a low,
soft voice

7. **fluent**
(flu´ ənt) *adj.*
spoken or written
smoothly

8. **banter**
(ban´ tər) *v.*
to joke playfully with
someone

9. **translate**
(trans´ lāt) *v.*
to change to another
language

10. **exclaim**
(eks klām´) *v.*
to cry out

The Human Voice

 Word Meanings

Definitions

 Write the vocabulary word next to its definition. Each word is used once.

1. To speak under your breath; to speak so quietly that almost no one can hear you _____

2. To tell something important, often to a large crowd of people who have been eagerly anticipating what you have to say

   _____

3. To lightheartedly joke back and forth with someone; to tease

   _____

4. Describes a spoken or written phrase that flows

   _____

5. To demand someone's presence, as if you are a king or queen; to send for_____

6. To shout loudly in surprise, joy, anger, or pain

   _____

7. To make a statement; to pronounce _____

8. To express admiration for and gratitude to someone who has done a good job _____

9. To express in one language what was said in another language

   _____

10. A comment that is harshly critical of another person; a hurtful remark _____

② Reference Skills

Dictionary Sentences

 Read each vocabulary word and the example sentences below. Write a check mark in the box of the sentence that correctly illustrates the meaning of the vocabulary word.

1. summon

☐ The queen *summoned* her counselors to her side.

☐ Don't *summon* so loudly—someone might hear you!

2. announce

☐ My friend and I like to *announce* back and forth.

☐ "It's a very fine day!" the White Rabbit *announced*.

3. translate

☐ His rude remark *translated* me.

☐ Can you *translate* that speech into English?

4. murmur

☐ You can hear students *murmuring* in the library.

☐ The principal *murmured* loudly into the microphone.

5. commend

☐ The general *commended* the soldiers on winning the battle.

☐ "It's eight o'clock," she *commended*.

6. utter

☐ *Uttering* is prohibited in the gymnasium.

☐ "Don't *utter* another word," demanded the teacher.

Vocabulary List

1. utter
2. summon
3. commend
4. insult
5. announce
6. murmur
7. fluent
8. banter
9. translate
10. exclaim

3 Build New Vocabulary

Noun Forms

 Write the noun form of the correct vocabulary word in each blank. The noun forms are shown in the box below. Each word is used only once.

commendation	announcement	fluency
translation	exclamation	

1. If you make good grades in school, you might receive a letter of

   _____ from your state senator for a job well done.

2. The English _____ of the French title *Le Petit Prince* is *The Little Prince*.

3. "Give me liberty, or give me death!" is a famous

   _____ by Patrick Henry, an American statesman who lived during the Revolutionary War.

4. Before you run for student council, you should make an

   _____ of your candidacy to inform the student body.

5. In order to deliver a speech with _____, it helps to practice it over and over again.

• •

Draw a line to match the beginning of each sentence with the ending that fits best.

6. If you are awarded a certificate for good citizenship, _____.

7. If you can speak a language effortlessly, _____.

8. "Ouch, that hurt!" _____.

9. Changing *bene* in Italian to *good* in English _____.

10. If you stand up to tell information, _____.

A. is a translation.

B. is an exclamation.

C. you are making an announcement.

D. you have received a commendation.

E. you have fluency.

Score _____ (Top Score 10)   The Human Voice • Build New Vocabulary

4 Word Play

Dialogue in a Play

 Read the lines and stage directions from the play below. Then write the vocabulary word that makes the most sense in each blank.

MESSENGER: Hamlet! The queen, your mother, has

_____ed you to her room! You must come at once!

HAMLET: Why do you _____ so loudly? I'm right behind you, and you have no need to shout.

MESSENGER: *(Wringing his hands and _____ing quietly to himself, almost whispering)* I'm sorry sir . . . I do apologize . . . I must learn to hold my tongue . . . oh my . . . please don't tell the queen. . . .

HAMLET: Well, I will go to the queen, for I have an important

_____ment to make: I believe my uncle has murdered my father, the king.

QUEEN: What is this? It sounds like playful

_____ing between old friends, but I fear that this conversation is far more serious.

HAMLET: *(Turning around suddenly, appearing surprised but calm and unafraid)* My queen, my mother, I never imagined I

would _____ these words, but I believe that Claudius my uncle has killed your husband, my father.

QUEEN: Hamlet! You _____ me with such hurtful remarks! Why would you accuse your uncle of this horrible crime?

HAMLET: I accuse my uncle in the name of truth, dear mother.

QUEEN: *(Turning her back on Hamlet)* Your words send daggers into

my heart. I called you to my room to _____ you for being so obedient and treating your uncle with respect. Now I will go straightway to tell him of your deceit.

Vocabulary Review

1 Review Word Meanings

Read the passage below. Then answer the questions about the boldfaced vocabulary words.

Women's Rights

In 1848, the first national women's rights **delegation** met in Seneca, New York. The **intention** was to begin a movement that would convince **politicians** to give women and men equal rights. This delegation's **viewpoint** was that women should not be **prohibited** from voting. They wanted **suffrage** for all women and the **elimination** of all inequalities between men and women.

Most men of that time did not like the **aggression** women displayed as they **publicly** argued with government officials and even broke the law so they could **plead** their case for equal rights before a judge. Some men thought the women's movement was a **conspiracy** against them. Others told their wives to stop being silly. Although women knew that the battle for equal rights would be long and **strenuous,** they may not have **calculated** that it would be another 70 years before Congress would pass a law giving them the right to vote.

Now read the following questions. Then completely fill in the bubble of the correct answer.

1. In which sentence is the word *prohibited* contrasted with its opposite meaning?
   - (A) Although women were prohibited from voting, men were prevented only from breaking the law.
   - (B) Although women were prohibited from voting, men were allowed full rights of citizenship.
   - (C) Although women were prohibited from voting, men were not pleased with the women's movement.

2. Which of the following is the correct definition of *delegation?*
   - (A) A group of people who represent other people
   - (B) A secret, illegal plan
   - (C) To give citizens the right to vote

3. What is the definition of *strenuous?*
   - (A) lasting for a short time
   - (B) making great progress
   - (C) requiring great effort

4. In which sentence is the word *publicly* used in the correct context?
   - (A) Some men publicly supported the women's movement.
   - (B) Some men publicly formed a conspiracy against the women's movement.
   - (C) Some men publicly met in secret to discuss the women's movement.

5. Which of the following words is a synonym of the word *viewpoint?*
   - (A) tower
   - (B) opinion
   - (C) intention

6. To "plead a case" means which of the following?
   - (A) to damage a case by giving too much information
   - (B) to ask a judge for forgiveness
   - (C) to argue the case in a court of law

② Review Word Meanings

Read the passage below. Then answer the questions about the boldfaced vocabulary words.

The Leaders

The leaders of the first national women's convention were Elizabeth Cady Stanton and Lucretia Mott. As they began to **coordinate** the women's movement, many women joined this national **alliance.** They felt that they could no longer **tolerate** men **dominating** them. Susan B. Anthony became a **comrade** of Stanton and Mott, and she was a strong **advocate** for women's rights. Although these women gave **fluent** speeches about their views, as soon as they would **utter** a word their **foes** would interrupt by **exclaiming** rude comments and shouting **insults** at them.

Now read the following questions. Then completely fill in the bubble of the correct answer.

1. Which dictionary sentence uses *insult* as it is used in the passage above?
   - Ⓐ She insults him too much.
   - Ⓑ The room smelled of insults.
   - Ⓒ The insults need to stop.

2. Which set of guide words would *comrade* come between?
   - Ⓐ compete/compound
   - Ⓑ compromise/concept
   - Ⓒ command/complex

3. Which of the following is a synonym for *foes?*
   - Ⓐ friends
   - Ⓑ forces
   - Ⓒ opponents

4. One definition of the word *advocate* is "a person who speaks out in favor of something." Which part of *advocate* is the Latin root that means "to call or speak"?
   - Ⓐ ad
   - Ⓑ voc
   - Ⓒ ate

5. Which of the following is a synonym of the word *comrade?*
   - Ⓐ friend
   - Ⓑ advocate
   - Ⓒ foe

6. Which of the following *is not* true according to the passage above?
   - Ⓐ Susan B. Anthony became a friend of Stanton and Mott.
   - Ⓑ Susan B. Anthony supported women's rights.
   - Ⓒ Very few women joined this national alliance.

7. Which set of guide words would *advocate* and *alliance* come between?
   - Ⓐ addition/almost
   - Ⓑ advice/alike
   - Ⓒ aerobic/alloy

8. Which of the following is the noun form of *tolerate?*
   - Ⓐ tolerantly
   - Ⓑ tolerating
   - Ⓒ toleration

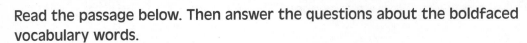

③ Review Word Meanings

Read the passage below. Then answer the questions about the boldfaced vocabulary words.

Equality

Although women won the right to vote in 1920, it was not until World War II that men were forced to **acknowledge** that women were just as capable as they were and should be free to **pursue** their career goals. The fact that six million women went to work to fill the jobs of military men clearly showed that women deserved equal treatment. Posters showing women working in factories became part of the **propaganda** designed to maintain support for the war effort. Women **enlisted** in the armed forces and were eager to **comply** with the rules of the military, just as men had done for many years. Some women inspected equipment; others **translated** information that was intercepted from enemy forces. Men no longer kept women from advancing in society, and many did their best to **accommodate** women in the workplace.

••

Now read the following questions. Then completely fill in the bubble of the correct answer.

1. To *acknowledge* something is to _____ that it is true.
   - Ⓐ complain
   - Ⓑ admit
   - Ⓒ reject

2. Which of the following is an antonym of *enlist?*
   - Ⓐ join
   - Ⓑ sign up
   - Ⓒ resist

3. In the passage, *accommodate* means which of the following?
   - Ⓐ make room for
   - Ⓑ challenge
   - Ⓒ tolerate

4. In which sentence is *comply* used in the correct context?
   - Ⓐ Women expected to comply information for the military.
   - Ⓑ Women had to comply their rights in 1920.
   - Ⓒ All citizens are expected to comply with the laws of this country.

5. Which is the correct definition of *propaganda?*
   - Ⓐ beliefs that are spread to gain supporters
   - Ⓑ beliefs that are kept hidden from others
   - Ⓒ beliefs that people in other countries don't share

6. What does it mean to *pursue* one's career goals?
   - Ⓐ to put them on hold
   - Ⓑ to follow them
   - Ⓒ to buy them

7. The prefix *com-*, as in *comply* and *comrade,* means _____.
   - Ⓐ with or together
   - Ⓑ against
   - Ⓒ before

8. According to the passage above, which statement is true?
   - Ⓐ Women won the right to vote in 1920.
   - Ⓑ Women could not fill men's jobs.
   - Ⓒ Women were not allowed to join the armed forces.

4 Review Word Meanings

Read the passage below. Then answer the questions about the boldfaced vocabulary words.

Women in Office

In July of 1984, Walter Mondale, the Democratic nominee for president, **summoned** reporters and **announced** that he had chosen Geraldine Ferraro as his running mate. Geraldine Ferraro became the first woman in American history to be **proposed** as a candidate for vice president. Although Mrs. Ferraro was a **cunning** and respected member of Congress known for her **interpersonal** skills, it was still a **compliment** for her to be chosen as the first female vice-presidential candidate. Mondale and Ferraro hoped that many women would cast their **ballots** for them at the **polls** on election day. However, Mondale was the **underdog** because he was running against Ronald Reagan, who was the current, popular president.

Now read the following questions. Then completely fill in the bubble of the correct answer.

1. In which sentence is *ballots* used correctly?
   - Ⓐ The ballots were filled with people waiting to vote.
   - Ⓑ The ballots were placed in a locked box.
   - Ⓒ The ballots announced the results of the election.

2. Which is the base word of *interpersonal?*
   - Ⓐ inter
   - Ⓑ person
   - Ⓒ personal

3. Which describes *compliment?*
   - Ⓐ positive comment
   - Ⓑ negative comment
   - Ⓒ neutral comment

4. Which word means "spoke softly"?
   - Ⓐ proposed
   - Ⓑ murmured
   - Ⓒ announced

5. In which sentence is the word *summoned* used in the correct context?
   - Ⓐ The candidate summoned her assistant.
   - Ⓑ The candidate summoned her speech.
   - Ⓒ The candidate summoned the television.

6. Which of the following is a synonym for *cunning?*
   - Ⓐ clever
   - Ⓑ charming
   - Ⓒ powerful

7. Which sentence provides the correct definition of *underdog?*
   - Ⓐ An underdog is a person who makes a great effort in a contest.
   - Ⓑ An underdog is a person who wins a contest.
   - Ⓒ An underdog is a person who is expected to lose a contest.

8. Which set below contains words that can all be used both as verbs and as adjectives?
   - Ⓐ cunning, murmured, announced
   - Ⓑ proposed, summoned, murmured
   - Ⓒ compliment, proposed, announced

Vocabulary List

1. crater
(krā´ tər) *n.*
large hole in the ground

2. universe
(ū´ nə vûrs´) *n.*
entire physical world

3. spectrum
(spek´ trəm) *n.*
band of colors that white light is separated into

4. astronomer
(ə stron´ ə mər) *n.*
scientist who studies heavenly bodies

5. constellation
(kon´ stə lā´ shən) *n.*
group of stars that form a pattern

6. comet
(kom´ it) *n.*
bright heavenly body made of ice and dust

7. satellite
(sat´ ə līt´) *n.*
object that orbits in space

8. revolve
(ri volv´) *v.*
to move in a circle around something else

9. celestial
(sə les´ chəl) *adj.*
relating to the sky

10. meteor
(mē´ tē ər) *n.*
shooting star

"Astronomy" Vocabulary

1 Word Meanings

Restating for Meaning

 Underline the part of each sentence that restates or gives the meaning of the boldfaced word.

1. An **astronomer** use telescopes and other instruments to study stars, planets, and other objects in the sky.

2. A **crater** on the moon is a huge, hollowed-out space that is visible from Earth.

3. Astronomers use a star's **spectrum** to study the star by breaking its light into separate bands of colors.

4. The **constellation** Orion is a pattern of stars that looks like a hunter.

5. Halley's **comet** is a mass of rock particles, ice, and gases with a tail that orbits the sun once each 76 years.

6. Earth's only **satellite** is the moon, a body that orbits Earth about every 27 days.

7. All the planets **revolve** around the sun, but they each circle it from a different distance.

8. When a piece of rock burns up in Earth's atmosphere, it is called a **meteor.**

9. Because the planets, stars, comets, and meteors are all objects located in the sky, they are called **celestial** bodies.

10. The universe, containing the entire physical world and all of its energy, is believed by scientists to still be growing outward.

Score _____ (Top Score 10)

2 Reference Skills

Using a Glossary

 Read the glossary entries in the box below. Then answer the questions about the entries.

---

u ni verse (ū´ nə vûrs´) *n.* **1.** all that exists, including Earth, the heavens, and all of space; entire physical world. **2.** an area or sphere of activity in its totality.

spec trum (spek´ trəm) *n., pl.* spectra or spectrums. a band of colors into which white light is separated according to wavelength by being passed through a prism or other material. The colors of the spectrum are red, orange, yellow, green, blue, indigo, and violet.

---

1. Which glossary entry has more than one meaning?

_____

2. What is the plural form of *spectrum?*

_____

3. The colors of a rainbow are the same as a

_____.

4. What part of speech are *spectrum* and *universe?*

_____

5. What is the phonetic spelling of *universe?*

_____

6. Where is a glossary located?

_____

Vocabulary List

1. crater

2. universe

3. spectrum

4. astronomer

5. constellation

6. comet

7. satellite

8. revolve

9. celestial

10. meteor

3 Build New Vocabulary

The Root *spec*

The following words all have the Latin root *spec*, which means "to look at" or "see." Match each word below with its correct definition. Use a dictionary if you need help.

1. _____ spectator

2. _____ respect

3. _____ spectacular

4. _____ inspect

A. forming an impressive or unusual sight

B. to look at closely and carefully

C. to view someone as having great value

D. a person who watches but does not take part

Use the words you matched above to complete the sentences below.

5. Astronomers who take the time and effort to share their knowledge and findings with us deserve our

_____.

6. Double rainbows are _____ to see because they have two awesome spectrums of color.

7. Watching meteors is a treat for the night sky

_____.

8. Space travel has given astronauts the chance to

_____ the craters on the moon.

Score _____ (Top Score 8)   "Astronomy" Vocabulary • Build New Vocabulary

4 Word Play

Similes

 Complete each simile below using one of the words from the word box.

celestial	revolve	spectrum
comet	satellite	constellation

1. Grains of sand are as numerous as the stars in a

   _____.

2. The skater began to _____ as quickly as
   a top.

3. My little brother hangs around me like a

   _____ around a planet.

4. The cans of paints were arranged as precisely as the colors in

   the _____.

5. My chances of making the team are as distant as a

   _____ body.

6. When Grandma calls me to dinner, I race like a

   _____ to the table.

• •

Think About It

Similes can bring poetry and other forms of creative writing to life.
Look around the room and think about the objects, people, and
actions you see that could be creatively described using similes.

Vocabulary List

1. **phenomenon**
   (fə nom′ ə non′) *n.*
   unusual thing or event

2. **illusion**
   (i loo′ zhən) *n.*
   a misleading
   appearance

3. **inquire**
   (in kwīr′) *v.*
   to ask; to seek
   information

4. **hunch**
   (hunch) *n.*
   a feeling or guess

5. **bewilder**
   (bi wil′ dər) *v.*
   to completely confuse
   or puzzle

6. **secrecy**
   (sē′ krə sē) *n.*
   keeping something
   from general
   knowledge

7. **suspense**
   (sə spens′) *n.*
   being undecided,
   worried, and in doubt

8. **suspect**
   (sə spekt′) *v.*
   to suppose something
   to be true

9. **deceive**
   (di sēv′) *v.*
   to lie or mislead

10. **eerie**
    (ir′ ē) *adj.*
    weird and frightening

The Mysterious Ocean

1 Word Meanings

Definition Examples

 Choose the vocabulary word that best matches the meaning of the boldfaced words in each sentence below.

1. A cuttlefish changes its color **to mislead** its predators into thinking it is part of the surroundings. _____

2. I became **totally confused** when she rattled off the directions to the dock. _____

3. It's just **a guess** that starfish and shellfish take breaks from the sun like people do. _____

4. **Strange and frightening** creatures move silently through the world of the deep sea. _____

5. The **unusual** giant kelp can grow three feet in a day.

   _____

6. To protect itself against predators, the porcupine fish swallows water, **making it look much larger than it actually is.**

   _____

7. When did you first **ask** about becoming an oceanographer?

   _____

8. When Maria discovered a diamond ring in the house, she **had a feeling** Pedro was going to marry her.

   _____

9. The spies were moving about quickly **to avoid being found.**

   _____

10. The detective novel ended leaving the reader **undecided** of who committed the crime. _____

2 Reference Skills

Suffix Definitions

Write each suffix beside its correct definition below. Use a dictionary for help.

suffixes:	-ment	-ive	-ly	-ful	-ness

1. full of _____

2. state of _____

3. like _____

4. condition or quality _____

5. the nature of _____

• •

Add the suffixes to the base words below. Write the new word in the blank. (**Hint:** If a word ends with *e*, the *e* is usually dropped before adding the suffix.)

6. bewilder + *-ment* = _____

7. eerie + *-ness* = _____

8. suspense + *-ful* = _____

9. inquire + *-ing* + *-ly* = _____

10. illusion + *-ive* = _____

• •

Match each new word from above to its definition below. Use a dictionary for help.

11. false or misleading *adj.* _____

12. full of uncertainty *adj.* _____

13. a condition that is strange and scary *n.* _____

14. in a questioning way *adv.* _____

15. the state of total confusion *n.* _____

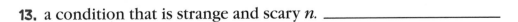

Vocabulary List

1. phenomenon

2. illusion

3. inquire

4. hunch

5. bewilder

6. secrecy

7. suspense

8. suspect

9. deceive

10. eerie

3 Build New Vocabulary

Context Clues

Read the passage below and fill in the appropriate vocabulary words using context clues.

The mysterious whale-sharks are the largest fish on Earth today. They can grow up to 50 feet in length—about the size of a large bus.

Their size and eating habits often _____, or mislead, people to believe that they are actually whales instead of sharks.

Even though every whale-shark has 300 rows of teeth hidden

under a fold of the skin, they _____ oceanographers by never chewing or biting their food. The whale-shark feeds by vacuuming and filtering plankton and small fish through its mouth and gills. The whale-shark's back is thick, tough, and covered with a series of white spots that give the

_____ to schools of fish that it is more of their group floating along. This is often their last mistake.

Very little is known about the reproduction of whale-sharks, but

researchers have a _____ that the young develop in egg cases that are held inside the mother's body until they are hatched. At birth, whale-sharks are only 40–50 centimeters long.

Western Australia is the only place in the world known to be regularly visited by the whale-sharks. Each year in March and April many young male whale-sharks appear. This

_____ probably occurs because of the coral growth. Thailand's coast offers divers a great opportunity to meet the whale-sharks. The white dots across the back of the shark form distinct lines and often mislead divers to incorrectly

_____ that they have seen the fierce tiger shark. Through laser-tracked tagging and captivity studies we hope to learn more about the mysterious ways of these gentle giants.

4 **Word Play**

Rhymes

 Write the vocabulary word that completes each rhyme below.

1. I've got a _____,
   Those fish in a bunch,
   Are going to be lunch!

2. After total confusion,
   I've come to the conclusion,

   That magic tricks are just an _____.

3. I have a theory,
   That being cheery,
   Makes people weary,

   Isn't that _____?

4. My paper was checked,
   There was a defect,
   I had to correct,
   It wasn't hard to perfect,
   My teacher will like it

   I _____.

• •

Now is your chance to earn two more points by writing a rhyme of your own. First choose a vocabulary word and brainstorm words that rhyme with your word. Then try some of your rhymes together until you find one you like. Write your rhyme in the space below.

_____

_____

_____

_____

_____

_____

1. dilemma
(di lem′ ə) *n.*
situation requiring a difficult choice

2. counsel
(koun′ səl) *n.*
advice or opinions

3. intervention
(in′ tər ven′ shən) *n.*
coming between opposing sides

4. alternative
(ôl tûr′ nə tiv) *n.*
a choice between things

5. clarity
(klar′ i tē) *n.*
being clear or understandable

6. arbitrary
(är′ bi trer′ ē) *adj.*
based on chance rather than reason

7. forum
(for′ əm) *n.*
a public meeting about problems

8. concession
(kən sesh′ ən) *n.*
granting or giving in

9. deadlock
(ded′ lok′) *n.*
a standstill

10. grievance
(grē′ vəns) *n.*
a wrong that causes unhappiness

Vocabulary for Problems

 **1** Word Meanings

Said With a Word

 Choose the vocabulary word that best matches the meaning of the underlined words in each sentence below.

1. Abraham Lincoln believed that the practice of slavery went against the Constitution, but <u>open meetings</u> in the South supported slavery. _____

2. President Lincoln wanted to <u>give advice</u> to the Southern states. _____

3. The South was faced with the <u>difficult choice</u> of working with Lincoln or leaving the Union. _____

4. The North and the South were at a <u>standstill</u>. _____

5. The federal government refused <u>to give in</u> to the South. _____

6. Many Southerners brought up other <u>complaints</u> they had with Lincoln. _____

7. Southerners could not tolerate the federal government <u>coming between them</u> in the matter of slavery, so they decided to form their own government. _____

8. Many Americans viewed the breaking away of the Southern states as an <u>unreasonable</u> act. _____

9. President Lincoln had no <u>choice</u> but to go to war with the Southern states. _____

10. Lincoln's famous Gettysburg Address is still <u>easily understood</u> nearly 150 years later. _____

Score _____ (Top Score 10) Vocabulary for Problems • Word Meanings

② Reference Skills

Defining Prefixes

Match each prefix to a definition below.

1. _____ twofold; twice; double

A. *re-*

2. _____ together; between or among

B. *con-*

3. _____ in association with; together

C. *be-*

4. _____ in association with; together

D. *inter-*

5. _____ again; back

E. *di-*

6. _____ throughout; about; to be

F. *com-*

• •

Use the definitions of the prefixes above to help you answer the questions about word meanings below. Write *Yes* or *No* in the blank.

7. Does *concession* mean "going along with something"?

_____

8. Does a *dilemma* involve more than one choice?

_____

9. Is there a need for *intervention* when people are cooperating?

_____

10. Does something that *revolves* only stay in one place?

_____

• •

 Think About It

Knowing prefixes and suffixes and their meanings will help you decode unfamiliar words.

Vocabulary List

1. dilemma
2. counsel
3. intervention
4. alternative
5. clarity
6. arbitrary
7. forum
8. concession
9. deadlock
10. grievance

3 Build New Vocabulary

Latin and Greek Words

Read each Greek or Latin word and its meaning. Write the related vocabulary word in the blank.

1. *cedere:* to yield or give in _____

2. *foris:* outside _____

3. *clarus:* bright, clear _____

4. *consulere:* to consult _____

5. *intervenire:* to come between _____

6. *arbitrarius:* uncertain _____

7. *di + lemma:* two assumptions _____

8. *alternus:* one after the other _____

• •

Use your new knowledge of Greek and Latin base words to answer the following questions. Write *Yes* or *No* in the blank.

9. Would a *counselor* consult? _____

10. Does *alter* mean "to change from one thing to another"?

_____

11. Is a *clarification* clearly understood?

_____

12. Can a *forum* be a secret meeting? _____

13. Is there always one easy answer in a *dilemma?*

_____

14. Is interrupting a type of *intervention?*

_____

15. Does *arbitrary* mean "certain" or

"sure of"? _____

Score _____ (Top Score 15)   Vocabulary for Problems • Build New Vocabulary

Word Play

Spoonerisms

Read the sentences with spoonerisms below. Rewrite the words correctly and underline the vocabulary word.

1. Be sure to speak slowly and carefully for the *cake* of *slarity.*

   _____

2. After dinner, we are meeting at the community building for

   fonight's torum. _____

3. Her *tounsel caught* us to think before we speak.

   _____

4. The students wrote their *prievance* on *gaper* and left it on their

   teacher's desk. _____

5. Eating a fresh garden salad was a *althy healternative* to our

   usual after school snack. _____

6. He is *druggling* with a *stilemma* between choosing art class

   and drama. _____

7. Our parents finally made a *thcession* after *coninking* about it

   all day. _____

8. The decision about building the *didge* was *breadlocked.*

   _____

1. **eternal**
   (i tûr´ nəl) *adj.*
   without beginning
   or end

2. **chronic**
   (kron´ ik) *adj.*
   lasting a long time

3. **indefinite**
   (in def´ ə nit) *adj.*
   not certain, not exact

4. **interval**
   (in´ tər vəl) *n.*
   time or space between

5. **prolong**
   (prə lông´) *v.*
   to extend in time

6. **decade**
   (dek´ ād) *n.*
   ten years

7. **cease**
   (sēs) *v.*
   to stop

8. **prior**
   (prī´ ər) *adj.*
   earlier

9. **continual**
   (kən tin´ ū əl) *adj.*
   goes on and on

10. **time-honored**
    (tīm´ on´ ərd) *adj.*
    respected for age
    or usage

"Time" Vocabulary

 Word Meanings

Extended Definitions

 Read the extended definitions and write the matching vocabulary word in the example sentence given.

1. *not clearly defined; no exact limits*

   My plans for the future are _____.

2. *earlier in time, order, or importance*

   I made plans _____ to hearing about her party.

3. *a period of ten years; a space between events*

   The ten-year-old theater will celebrate a _____

   of business during the thirty-minute _____ between acts.

4. *time without beginning or end; to cause to come to an end*

   The circle is _____ because it neither ends nor begins.

5. *revered, respected, or observed because of age or long usage*

   The Hawaiian cliff-diving ceremony is a

   _____ tradition.

6. *lasting a long time; coming back again and again*

   My brother suffers from _____ asthma.

7. *to make longer, especially in time; to extend*

   Our principal will _____ our recess.

8. *continuing without a break; continuous*

   The dog's _____ barking woke us up.

② Reference Skills

Phonetic Spellings

Circle the correct pronunciation spelling for each vocabulary word below. Use the pronunciation key to help you.

/a/, **a**t; /ā/, l**a**te; /â/, c**a**re; /ä/, f**a**ther; /e/, s**e**t; /ē/, m**e**;
/i/, **i**t; /ī/, k**i**te; /o/, **o**x; /ō/, r**o**se; /ô/, br**ou**ght, r**a**w; /oi/, c**oi**n; /o͝o/,
b**oo**k; /o͞o/, t**oo**; /or/, f**or**m; /ou/, **ou**t; /u/, **u**p; /yo͞o/, c**u**be; /ûr/,
t**ur**n, g**er**m, l**ear**n, f**ir**m, w**or**k; /ə/, **a**bout, chick**e**n, penc**i**l, cann**o**n,
circ**u**s; /ch/, **ch**air; /hw/, **wh**ich; /ng/, ri**ng**; /sh/, **sh**op; /th/, **th**in;
/ᴕ/, **th**ere; /zh/, trea**s**ure

1. eternal	i tûr´ nəl	i tûr´ nāl	ē tûr´ nəl
2. chronic	kron´ ich	kron īk´	kron´ ik
3. prolong	prə lənj´	prə lông´	prəl´ ông
4. indefinite	in def´ ə nit	in´ də f ə nit	in dē fə´ nit
5. interval	intər´ vəl	in´ tər vāl	in´ tər vəl
6. time-honored	tīm´ on´ ərd	tim´ ən´ erd	tīm´ hon ər
7. cease	cēs	sēs	ses
8. continual	kən tin´ yo͞o əl	kon tin´ yo͞o əl	kən tin´ yo͞o el
9. prior	prī´ or	prī´ er	prī´ ər
10. decade	deck´ād	dek´ād	dek´aid

• •

💡 Think About It

Learning how to identify phonetic spelling symbols can help build your vocabulary skills. Knowing the difference between (kon´ tent) and (kən tent´) when you see the word *content* will clarify how you should *say* the word and *what it means.*

Vocabulary List

1. eternal
2. chronic
3. indefinite
4. interval
5. prolong
6. decade
7. cease
8. prior
9. continual
10. time-honored

3 Build New Vocabulary

The Prefix *in-*

 Add the prefix *in-* to each word below. Then write the definition of the new word without using the base word. Use the dictionary if you need help.

1. cautious _____

   _____

2. capable _____

   _____

3. comparable _____

   _____

4. competent _____

   _____

5. considerate _____

   _____

6. decisive _____

   _____

7. dependent _____

   _____

8. fertile _____

   _____

9. frequent _____

   _____

10. voluntary _____

    _____

4 **Word Play**

Informal Language

 Match the vocabulary word to the correct informal-language phrase.

1. _____ drag one's feet

2. _____ twenty-four seven

3. _____ put a lid on it

4. _____ forever and a day

5. _____ keep someone hanging

A. indefinite

B. eternal

C. continual

D. cease

E. prolong

• •

 Use the informal-language phrase from above to complete each sentence below.

6. Many convenience stores are open

_____.

7. The bus ride on our field trip seemed to last

_____.

8. If you want someone to stop talking, you could say,

" _____ ".

9. When one does not make definite plans to meet another person, he or she

_____.

10. It is not good to _____
when doing homework because it might not be completed
on time.

Vocabulary List

1. **thwart**
   (thwort) *v.*
   to prevent from doing
   something

2. **half-mast**
   (haf´ mast´) *n.*
   a flag's midway
   position to represent
   mourning

3. **flaw**
   (flô) *n.*
   an imperfection

4. **deficiency**
   (di fish´ ən sē) *n.*
   a lack

5. **abnormal**
   (ab nor´ məl) *adj.*
   different from
   the usual

6. **disrupt**
   (dis rupt´) *v.*
   to upset or break up

7. **impair**
   (im pâr´) *v.*
   to damage or weaken

8. **approximate**
   (ə prok´ sə mit) *adj.*
   nearly correct

9. **vague**
   (vāg) *adj.*
   not clear

10. **scarce**
    (skârs) *adj.*
    difficult to get or find

Not Quite

 **1** **Word Meanings**

Word Choice

 Choose the word from the Vocabulary List that correctly completes each sentence below.

1. The *Titanic* had one _____, or imperfection; there were not enough lifeboats on board.

2. When a national tragedy occurs all American flags should be flown at _____ instead of full-mast.

3. Natural blue diamonds are _____, or hard to find.

4. If you receive _____ directions to a house, it is very likely that you will get lost.

5. If your doctor tells you that you have an iron _____, you may look tired and lack energy.

6. Brocoflower is an _____ looking vegetable.

7. Listening to loud music will _____, or damage, your hearing.

8. In comic books, superheroes try to _____ the plans of villains.

9. When people talk aloud at a movie, they _____ other people's enjoyment.

10. An estimation is an _____ answer.

② Reference Skills

Related Word Forms

 Circle the correct word form in the sentence and write the related vocabulary word in the blank.

1. She (vaguely, disruption) remembered him saying that he

would be late. _____

2. The store gave me an (scarcely, approximation) of the total cost

to fix my stereo. _____

3. A diet (deficient, abnormality) in vitamins can lead to illness.

_____

4. Her shyness was an (flawless, impairment) to her public

speaking. _____

5. The road construction outside our classroom was (disruptive,

approximately). _____

6. The critics loved this movie and said it was (deficiently, flawlessly)

made. _____

7. Pollutants in river waters often cause death or (vagueness,
abnormalities) in the fish living there.

_____

8. During the Great Depression, recreational money was a
(scarcity, impairment).

_____

Vocabulary List

1. thwart

2. half-mast

3. flaw

4. deficiency

5. abnormal

6. disrupt

7. impair

8. approximate

9. vague

10. scarce

3 Build New Vocabulary

Building Adverbs

Change each adjective below into an adverb by adding *-ly*.

1. scarce _____

2. deficient _____

3. abnormal _____

4. approximate _____

5. disruptive _____

6. vague _____

Complete each sentence below using the correct adverb from above.

7. The weather during the drought of the 1930s was

_____ dry.

8. It was impossible for the farmers to tell

_____ how long the drought would last.

9. The topsoil had been _____ protected from being blown away by the wind.

10. _____ any farmers survived the drought as most were forced to seek jobs in other places.

11. The witness _____ described what he thought he saw during the accident.

12. The young child _____ entered the room and interrupted our parent-teacher conference.

4   Word Play

Silly Rhymes

 Read the poems below. Complete each poem by writing the related vocabulary word in the blank.

1. My grandpa from Utah

   is an outlaw.

   That's his only _____.

2. That nail over there

   might _____

   the tire on my wheelchair.

3. The rough waves may _____

   the smooth escort

   of the ship to its port.

4. I added an egg,

   some nutmeg,

   and a chicken leg,

   because my recipe

   was _____.

5. My dog Orvil

   took me to the formal.

   His tuxedo looked great,

   but he smelled _____.

Vocabulary Review

1 Review Word Meanings

Read the passage below. Then answer the questions about the boldfaced vocabulary words.

Observations by Astronomers

Thousands of years ago, early **astronomers** noticed that stars seemed to form patterns. They gave each pattern, or **constellation,** a name such as The Big Dipper. However, these early astronomers were **bewildered** by the sudden and seemingly **arbitrary** appearance of other **celestial** bodies. They had no idea that the **phenomenon** they called a shooting star was actually a **meteor** burning up in Earth's atmosphere.

By the 1400s, more scientific observations about the **universe** were made. In 1682, Edmond Halley calculated the **approximate interval** between the appearances of a **comet.** Halley's comet now bears his name.

Now read the following questions. Then completely fill in the bubble of the correct answer.

1. Which of the following words includes a prefix that means "between"?
   Ⓐ bewilder
   Ⓑ constellation
   Ⓒ interval

2. Which of these sentences includes a restatement that defines *constellation?*
   Ⓐ A constellation is a pattern of stars that can often look like an animal.
   Ⓑ A constellation always has one star that is much brighter than the others.
   Ⓒ Many constellations were named by astronomers who lived thousands of years ago.

3. Which definition correctly defines *meteor?*
   Ⓐ masses of rock particles, ice, and gases that orbit the sun
   Ⓑ celestial bodies that orbit planets
   Ⓒ pieces of rock that burn up as they enter Earth's atmosphere

4. In which sentence is *bewildered* used in the correct context?
   Ⓐ Early astronomers bewildered meteors and called them "shooting stars."
   Ⓑ Early astronomers observed meteors as they bewildered in the sky.
   Ⓒ Early astronomers were bewildered by the sudden appearance of meteors.

5. Which of the following is an extended definition for a *phenomenon?*
   Ⓐ a bright, heavenly body made of ice, frozen gases, and dust particles, and having a long, visible tail that points away from the sun
   Ⓑ a person or a thing that is extraordinary or remarkable
   Ⓒ to confuse or puzzle completely

6. Which of the following words is a synonym for *celestial?*
   Ⓐ glowing
   Ⓑ heavenly
   Ⓒ revolving

② Review Word Meanings

Read the passage below. Then answer the questions about the boldfaced vocabulary words.

Galileo Galilei

In the early 1600s, Galileo Galilei designed a telescope that allowed him to see with **clarity** the **craters** of Earth's moon and the four moons, which he called **satellites,** of Jupiter. Galileo also published a book that helped prove Copernicus's idea that the planets **revolve** around the sun and not Earth. This view was a **grievance** to the leaders of the Catholic church and they ordered him to support the Earth-centered idea.

Then the pope made a **concession** that Galileo could write as long as he didn't go against church beliefs. Faced with this **dilemma,** Galileo found he was unable to comply. The pope decided that **intervention** was necessary. Galileo was put on trial, found guilty, and placed under house arrest for the rest of his life. He had no **alternative** but to continue his work in **secrecy.**

Now read the following questions. Then completely fill in the bubble of the correct answer.

1. Which of the following words includes a prefix that means "together"?
   Ⓐ alternative
   Ⓑ dilemma
   Ⓒ compatible

2. What is the correct definition of *alternative?*
   Ⓐ the act of coming between two or more things
   Ⓑ a choice between two or more things
   Ⓒ the act of agreeing with two or more things

3. Which word has a prefix that means "again"?
   Ⓐ revolve
   Ⓑ alternative
   Ⓒ concession

4. What word is an antonym for *clarity?*
   Ⓐ understanding
   Ⓑ clearness
   Ⓒ confusion

5. Which word includes a prefix that has the meaning "two"?
   Ⓐ dilemma
   Ⓑ intervention
   Ⓒ concession

6. Which is the correct definition of *grievance?*
   Ⓐ sorrow so great that it cannot be expressed
   Ⓑ a real or imagined wrong that causes distress
   Ⓒ the act of giving in to someone or something

7. What is the adverb form of *alternative?*
   Ⓐ alternate
   Ⓑ alternatively
   Ⓒ alternation

8. Which of the following is an example of a *satellite?*
   Ⓐ meteor
   Ⓑ crater
   Ⓒ moon

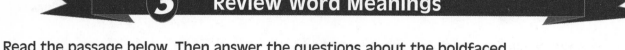

3 Review Word Meanings

Read the passage below. Then answer the questions about the boldfaced vocabulary words.

Hubble Space Telescope

More than 300 years after Galileo's discoveries, in a moment full of **suspense,** the Hubble Space Telescope was launched from the space shuttle *Discovery* in 1990. Unfortunately, the plan for the telescope to take photographs as it orbited Earth was **thwarted.** Instead of sharp photographs, the telescope sent photos that showed only **vague** and **indefinite** images of the stars and planets.

At first, scientists did not know what **impaired** the Hubble Telescope. Then they discovered that a **deficiency** in one of its mirrors did not provide enough light to form clear images. This was a **chronic** problem that continued to **disrupt** photos until a team of astronauts repaired the **abnormal** mirror in 1993.

Now read the following questions. Then completely fill in the bubble of the correct answer.

1. The plan for the telescope to take photographs as it orbited Earth was *thwarted,* or _____.
   - Ⓐ successful
   - Ⓑ obstructed
   - Ⓒ wonderful

2. What word is an antonym of *abnormal?*
   - Ⓐ usual
   - Ⓑ rare
   - Ⓒ lacking

3. In which of the following sentences is *vague* used in the correct context?
   - Ⓐ The vague telescope took photographs that showed distant stars as bright objects.
   - Ⓑ The telescope took photographs that showed vague stars as bright objects.
   - Ⓒ The telescope took photographs that showed distant stars as bright objects with vague shapes.

4. Which is the correct definition of *impair?*
   - Ⓐ to damage or make weak
   - Ⓑ to put into pairs
   - Ⓒ to make correct

5. What is it called when one is eagerly waiting for a mystery to be explained?
   - Ⓐ interval
   - Ⓑ dilemma
   - Ⓒ suspense

6. The prefix *in-* in the word *indefinite* means _____.
   - Ⓐ *very* definite
   - Ⓑ *not* definite
   - Ⓒ *between* definite

7. If something is *chronic,* it _____.
   - Ⓐ is unclear
   - Ⓑ occurs again and again
   - Ⓒ is damaged

8. Which of the following words includes a prefix that means "not"?
   - Ⓐ impair
   - Ⓑ indefinite
   - Ⓒ both A and B

4 Review Word Meanings

Read the passage below. Then answer the questions about the boldfaced vocabulary words.

The Sun

Although space seem to go on indefinitely, telescopes like the Hubble have allowed scientists to observe stars that have every color of the **spectrum.** Our sun is actually a star, and although it gives the **illusion** of being fairly close to Earth, it is approximately 93,000,000 miles away.

Many people think that the sun is **eternal,** but it is a middle-aged star that will first expand, use up its fuel, and then finally collapse. When the sun begins to use up its fuel, its rays will **cease** going through the clouds in Earth's atmosphere and Earth will gradually become very cold. The fact that our sun will eventually die and that there is nothing that will **prolong** its life is an **eerie** thought.

Now read the following questions. Then completely fill in the bubble of the correct answer.

1. Which of the following words includes a Latin root that means "to see"?
   - Ⓐ illusion
   - Ⓑ eternal
   - Ⓒ spectrum

2. Which of the following is the correct definition of *cease?*
   - Ⓐ to end
   - Ⓑ stop
   - Ⓒ both A and B

3. What is the base word of *prolong?*
   - Ⓐ pro
   - Ⓑ long
   - Ⓒ prolong

4. Which of the following sentences uses *spectrum* in the correct context?
   - Ⓐ A spectrum breaks white light into a prism of colors.
   - Ⓑ A prism breaks white light into a spectrum of colors.
   - Ⓒ A prism breaks spectrum light into different colors.

5. Many people think that the sun is *eternal,* or that it _____.
   - Ⓐ will end soon
   - Ⓑ has healing powers
   - Ⓒ has no beginning or end

6. If something is *eternal,* it is _____.
   - Ⓐ forever
   - Ⓑ annoying
   - Ⓒ becoming smaller

7. Which of the following is the correct definition of *eerie?*
   - Ⓐ not real
   - Ⓑ having no limits
   - Ⓒ strange and frightening

8. Which of the following means the opposite of *illusion?*
   - Ⓐ reality
   - Ⓑ mistake
   - Ⓒ imagination

Vocabulary List

1. **genetic**
   (jə net' ik) *adj.*
   relating to traits
   passed down
   from birth

2. **emancipation**
   (i man' sə pā' shən) *n.*
   freedom granted

3. **citizenship**
   (sit' ə zən ship') *n.*
   being a member of
   a country who has
   full rights

4. **nomad**
   (nō' mad) *n.*
   wanderer who has
   no permanent home

5. **ancestry**
   (an' ses trē) *n.*
   the past generations
   of family

6. **foreigner**
   (for' ə nər) *n.*
   a non-native person

7. **inscription**
   (in skrip' shən) *n.*
   special writing

8. **possessions**
   (pə zesh' ənz) *n.*
   things that are held
   or owned

9. **inheritance**
   (in her' i təns) *n.*
   things passed down
   from relatives

10. **destiny**
    (des' tə nē) *n.*
    the events that
    happen to a person

"Heritage" Vocabulary

 Word Meanings

Definitions

 Fill in the letter of the correct definition for each boldfaced vocabulary word in the sentences below.

A. freedom granted	**G.** non-native people
B. things passed down	**H.** a wanderer without a permanent home
C. what happens to a person	**I.** having legal rights as a member of a country
D. things that are owned	
E. special writings	**J.** the past generations of family
F. relating to traits passed down from birth	

1. ☐ During prehistoric times, nomads who had **roamed** the African desert for many years settled in the fertile Nile Valley.

2. ☐ Much of what we know about ancient Egypt is preserved on **inscriptions** carved on pharaohs' burial chamber walls.

3. ☐ The pharaohs believed that it was their **destiny** to live again after their deaths, so they had their bodies preserved.

4. ☐ Most pharaohs could trace their **ancestry** back to other pharaohs who had lived hundreds of years before them.

5. ☐ Many pharaohs were buried with gold funeral masks, jewels, valuable figurines, and other family **possessions.**

6. ☐ Ancient Egyptian women had many rights of **citizenship,** including the rights to own property and to have jobs.

7. ☐ Women also had the right to keep any **inheritance** that was left to them by their relatives.

8. ☐ Most Egyptian slaves were never granted their freedom, but occasionally a few were awarded their **emancipation** after years of faithful service.

9. ☐ After the twelfth century B.C., Egyptian power declined because Egypt was frequently invaded by **foreigners.**

10. ☐ Throughout its 3,000-year history, Egypt was ruled by many royal families that had no **genetic** relationship to one another.

2 Reference Skills

Base Words

 Read the base words in the first box, and locate each word's definition in the second box. Then fill in the correct base word and definition for each vocabulary word below. Use a dictionary if necessary.

Base Words	Definitions
foreign	writing
possess	determines characteristics
script	to have or own
inherit	from another country
gene	get from deceased ancestors

1. *inscription* Base _____

   Definition _____

2. *genetic* Base _____

   Definition _____

3. *possession* Base _____

   Definition _____

4. *foreigner* Base _____

   Definition _____

5. *inheritance* Base _____

   Definition _____

• •

 Think About It

You might be able to figure out the general meaning of an unfamiliar word if you recognize the base word.

Vocabulary List

1. genetic

2. emancipation

3. citizenship

4. nomad

5. ancestry

6. foreigner

7. inscription

8. possessions

9. inheritance

10. destiny

3 Build New Vocabulary

Word Origins

 Write each vocabulary word next to its origin. Then write each origin's definition from the box below. Use a dictionary to check your answers if necessary.

to go before	born
city	one's future; fate
owner	outside
to write	to release

1. Latin, *antecedere:* _____

_____

2. Greek, *genes:* _____

_____

3. Latin, *emancipare:* _____

_____

4. French, *destinee:* _____

_____

5. Latin, *heres:* _____

_____

6. Latin, *scribere:* _____

_____

7. Latin, *foris:* _____

_____

8. French, *cité:* _____

_____

4 **Word Play**

Is It Possible?

 Write *Yes* or *No* in the blank to tell whether each relationship is possible.

1. Can a foreigner have possessions? _____

2. Does a nomad have citizenship? _____

3. Is ancestry genetic? _____

4. Can an inscription be a destiny? _____

5. Can emancipation be an inheritance? _____

6. Do possessions have ancestry? _____

7. Can an inheritance be a destiny? _____

8. Can a foreigner have citizenship right away? _____

9. Can emancipation be a destiny? _____

10. Are descendants genetically related? _____

11. Can you have possessions from your ancestry? _____

12. Is citizenship genetic? _____

13. Could your inheritance be inscriptions? _____

14. Could a foreigner be a nomad? _____

15. Do you receive inscriptions after achieving citizenship? _____

● ●

 For 1 extra point, write your own question using at least two vocabulary words. Make sure the answer is either *Yes* or *No*.

_____

_____

_____

_____

"Good Traits" Vocabulary

Vocabulary List

1. **ambitious**
   (am bish′ əs) *adj.*
   strongly driven
   or eager

2. **compassion**
   (kəm pash′ ən) *n.*
   thoughtfulness,
   pity, sympathy

3. **poise**
   (poiz) *n.*
   a calm manner

4. **confidence**
   (kon′ fi dəns) *n.*
   faith in oneself,
   assurance

5. **evenhanded**
   (ē′ vən han′ did) *adj.*
   fair, just

6. **gracious**
   (grā′ shəs) *adj.*
   kind and polite

7. **integrity**
   (in teg′ ri tē) *n.*
   honor, honesty

8. **foresight**
   (for′ sīt′) *n.*
   looking or thinking
   ahead

9. **shrewd**
   (shrood) *adj.*
   clever, especially in
   practical matters

10. **virtuous**
    (vûr′ choo əs) *adj.*
    righteous, good

① Word Meanings

Synonyms

 Write a vocabulary word next to each pair of synonyms below.

1. fair, just _____

2. driven, eager _____

3. kind, courteous _____

4. honesty, honor _____

5. calmness, stability _____

6. assurance, boldness _____

7. clever, wise _____

8. upright, good _____

9. pity, sympathy _____

10. preparing, looking ahead _____

• •

 Write the letter of the correct definition in the blank beside each vocabulary word below.

11. _____ poise

12. _____ gracious

13. _____ shrewd

14. _____ compassion

15. _____ ambitious

A. clever or keen in practical matters

B. sympathy with desire to help others

C. a calm, confident manner

D. showing strong drive to achieve
or succeed

E. having or showing kindness
and courtesy

② Reference Skills

Using Antonyms

Read each sentence below and fill in the missing vocabulary word. (**Hint:** The antonym for each vocabulary word appears below the blank.) Use a thesaurus, if necessary.

1. Preparing before speaking in public will help you build

   _____ in yourself and in what you
   (self-doubt)

   have to say.

2. Having the _____ to research your topic
   (hindsight)

   well and practice your speech before giving it to an audience is a
   very good idea.

3. Starting your speech off with a humorous quote or a joke is a

   _____ way to grab your audience's
   (dull)

   attention.

4. Most people respect the courage it takes to speak in public and

   will be _____ audience members even if
   (rude)

   they disagree with the views of the speaker.

5. If you are an _____ student, you may want
   (lazy)

   to research a topic that interests you and ask your teacher if you
   could practice your public speaking skills by presenting this
   information to your class.

• •

 Think About It

Keep in mind that many antonyms do not mean *exactly* the opposite of the entry word. They may vary in degrees such as shown on a linear graph.

Vocabulary List

1. ambitious
2. compassion
3. poise
4. confidence
5. evenhanded
6. gracious
7. integrity
8. foresight
9. shrewd
10. virtuous

3 Build New Vocabulary

Hyphenated Compound Words

Combine the words in the box to form twelve compound words that match the definitions below. Some words will be used more than once.

best	hand	play
centered	held	season
class	limits	second
confident	middle	self
even	off	tempered

1. _____: made to fit and be used in the hand

2. _____: previously used by someone else

3. _____: next to the best

4. _____: calm; not easily upset

5. _____: not the busy time of the year

6. _____: having faith in one's own abilities

7. _____: concentrating on one's own self

8. _____: a game played to break a tie

9. _____: not a place to be entered; out of bounds

10. _____: part of social and economic class

11. _____: less than the first or best class

12. _____: a pass to a nearby teammate

• •

 Think About It

Even though most compound words combine the meanings of the word parts, some hold an entirely new meaning when combined. For example, *brainstorm* does not literally mean a storm in one's brain. Can you think of any others?

Score _____ (Top Score 12)   "Good Traits" Vocabulary • Build New Vocabulary

Word Play

Riddles

Answer each riddle below with a vocabulary word.

1. The Statue of Liberty stands for freedom
and equality. Since she has this "balanced"
view, you could say she is this.

_____

2. If you're wise enough to advise,
recognize, realize, and theorize,
then you'd be viewed as being this, I conclude.

_____

3. I calm the soul, with self-control.
I'm a trait that's not nervous or late.
What am I?

_____

4. There's no doubt about it.
This will help you take a stance,
and make an entrance with assurance.

_____

5. I've got things to do,
and places to go,
don't say I'm lazy,
it's just not so!
What am I?

_____

1. **astonish**
(ə ston′ ish) *v.*
to greatly surprise,
amaze

2. **exquisite**
(ek skwiz′ it) *adj.*
of great beauty
or perfection

3. **exceptional**
(ek sep′ shə nəl) *adj.*
very unusual

4. **exclusive**
(ek sklōō′ siv) *adj.*
open to only a few

5. **exotic**
(eg zot′ ik) *adj.*
foreign and strangely
beautiful

6. **atrocious**
(ə trō′ shəs) *adj.*
very bad

7. **outrageous**
(out rā′ jəs) *adj.*
shocking

8. **luminous**
(lōō′ mə nəs) *adj.*
shining

9. **notable**
(nō′ tə bəl) *adj.*
worthy of notice

10. **utmost**
(ut′ mōst′) *adj.*
of the greatest degree

Outstanding Words

1 **Word Meanings**

Exaggeration

 Fill in each blank with a vocabulary word that fits the exaggeration.

1. I will _____ them so much that when their mouths open, their jaws will hit the floor.

2. The unusual creature was so _____ that it must have been from another planet.

3. The club was so _____, nobody was good enough to belong.

4. Her hairdo was just _____; it looked like she had combed it with an eggbeater.

5. He tried his _____ to keep his mouth shut, but his tongue had a mind of its own.

6. The rest of us were wearing rags compared to her

    _____ dress.

7. The smell was so _____, our noses fell off our faces and ran away.

8. His _____ fluorescent flashlight could be seen for miles.

9. Her _____ performance was so unusual we were left speechless for days.

10. The child's story was a _____ success. He was ready for retirement at the age of ten.

2 Reference Skills

Multiple Meanings

Read the dictionary entry for each word. Then complete each sentence below using one of the words. Write the number of the definition you use on the blank after each sentence.

exclusive *adj.* **1.** limited to control by a single person or group: *The owner of the house has exclusive rights to the beach.* **2.** open to only a select few: *My brother belongs to an exclusive sailing club.* **3.** complete: *I will give this matter my exclusive attention.*

exquisite *adj.* **1.** of great beauty or perfection: *She had an exquisite face.* **2.** of great excellence or high quality: *The well-made chair showed my uncle's exquisite workmanship.* **3.** intensely sharp, keen: *She took exquisite delight in telling about her new baby brother.*

luminous *adj.* **1.** sending out its own light, shining: *The luminous fireflies were scattered about the yard.* **2.** full of light, bright: *It was late and the kitchen was the only luminous room of the house.* **3.** easily understood: *His plan was so luminous that even the young children understood it.*

1. The U.S. government has _____ ownership of Buck Island, which is just a few miles away from St. Croix. _____

2. Natives of the islands perform _____ stunts on their surfboards. _____

3. The slow pace of island life is a _____ idea that many people like. _____

4. Rare species of birds, butterflies, and _____ flowers live in the Blue Mountains of Jamaica. _____

5. The _____ morning sun over the water is an unforgettable sight. _____

Vocabulary List

1. astonish
2. exquisite
3. exceptional
4. exclusive
5. exotic
6. atrocious
7. outrageous
8. luminous
9. notable
10. utmost

 3 Build New Vocabulary

The Prefix ex-

 Write the letter of the correct definition in the blank beside each word below.

1. _____ expected   **A.** to travel over new land

2. _____ exquisite   **B.** from another country

3. _____ extensive   **C.** stretched out

4. _____ excellent   **D.** counted on happening

5. _____ exotic   **E.** superior, very good

6. _____ exceptional   **F.** keeping some out

7. _____ explore   **G.** of great beauty

8. _____ exclusive   **H.** very unusual

• •

 Use the words above to complete the following sentences.

9. The Caribbean islands are home to many

_____ birds, as well as rare and beautiful flowering plants.

10. The Hope Gardens in Jamaica are notable for their

_____ green lawns, magnificent palms, and gorgeous flowers.

11. In addition to the numerous campsites and inns in Jamaica, there are many expensive hotels and

_____ resorts.

12. Those who _____ the deep inland forests will be treated to the sounds of the shrieking parrots.

 Word Play

Tongue Twisters

 Use the vocabulary words to complete each tongue twister below.

1. Lovely, _____ lanterns lit the low-lying land.

2. Nearly ninety new _____ nurses were acknowledged for their knowledge.

3. The _____ actions of the aggressive alligator amazed all of us.

4. Eleven _____ Egyptians exchanged elaborate ebony etchings.

5. An engineer escorted an excellent executive to an

   _____ elevator.

6. Is it _____ to offer an octopus an orange?

7. Ezra exposed an extraordinary and _____ example of exaggeration.

8. Unless this unusual undertaking is given

   _____ effort, it will be unsuccessful.

9. Elaina's _____ evening gown was the envy of everyone at Ernie's entertaining event.

10. Alexander would always _____ his audience with his abstract art.

Vocabulary List

1. **outlook**
(out´ lŏŏk´) *n.*
point of view

2. **conspicuous**
(kən spik´ ū əs) *adj.*
attracting attention

3. **superficial**
(sōō pər fish´ əl) *adj.*
relating to or being
located on the surface

4. **receptive**
(ri sep´ tiv) *adj.*
open to new ideas
or suggestions

5. **assumption**
(ə sump´ shən) *n.*
something supposed
to be true

6. **resemble**
(ri zem´ bəl) *v.*
to be similar to

7. **obstruct**
(əb strukt´) *v.*
to block or prevent
passage

8. **perception**
(pər sep´ shən) *n.*
awareness,
observation

9. **recognize**
(rek´ əg nīz´) *v.*
to be aware of, to
understand clearly

10. **obvious**
(ob´ vē əs) *adj.*
easily seen or
understood

How You See It

 1 Word Meanings

Choosing Words

 Circle the vocabulary word that best completes
each sentence below.

1. In the fifteenth century, artists began to develop a new
(outlook / assumption) on the world around them.

2. This era, called the Renaissance, is *(resembled / recognized)* as
one of the greatest periods in the history of art.

3. The work of Renaissance artists was based on the
(obvious / assumption) that art should look like real life.

4. Michelangelo was *(conspicuous / receptive)* to the idea of
realistic art.

5. It soon became *(receptive / obvious)* that Michelangelo was a
truly gifted sculptor.

6. He and other artists, such as Leonardo da Vinci and Boticelli,
wanted their artwork to *(resemble / recognize)* that of the
Ancient Greeks and Romans.

7. Leonardo da Vinci had such fine *(perception / assumption)* of
the human body that his paintings are still considered to be
nearly perfect.

8. Before the Renaissance, many artists painted portraits that had
only a *(conspicuous / superficial)* likeness to the actual people.

9. Michelangelo designed the dome of St. Peter's Church, which is
still a *(conspicuous / superficial)* sight in Rome.

10. The dome, which rises more than 400 feet from the ground, is
so large that it *(outlooks / obstructs)* the view of the buildings
behind it.

2 Reference Skills

Dictionary Definitions

 Write each vocabulary word next to its dictionary definition or definitions below.

1. _____ *n.* **1.** a view into the future
   2. a point of view **3.** a place from which a view is obtained
   4. the view from a place

2. _____ *n.* **1.** something taken for granted or supposed to be true

3. _____ *adj.* attracting attention

4. _____ *adj.* open to new ideas or suggestions

5. _____ *v.* to be similar to

6. _____ *n.* **1.** observation; awareness
   2. depth of understanding; insight

7. _____ *adj.* **1.** easily seen or understood
   2. without hiding

8. _____ *v.* **1.** to know **2.** to identify
   3. to realize **4.** to take notice of as having the right to speak
   5. to show appreciation for

9. _____ *adj.* **1.** relating to or located on the surface **2.** lacking depth

10. _____ *v.* **1.** to block or be in the way of
    2. to interfere with the progress of something

● ●

Think About It

Many words are used in different ways at different times. Knowing an extended definition of a word and its different meanings will help build your vocabulary skills.

Vocabulary List

1. outlook
2. conspicuous
3. superficial
4. receptive
5. assumption
6. resemble
7. obstruct
8. perception
9. recognize
10. obvious

3 Build New Vocabulary

Closed Compound Words

 Write each closed compound word from the box next to its definition. Use a dictionary for support.

vineyard	superscript	shortchange
tiresome	freethinker	pushover
overtake	keepsake	marketplace
outstanding	outlook	overrated

1. something kept to remind someone of its original owner

   _____

2. an area where grapes are grown _____

3. a person who forms independent opinions

   _____

4. to catch up with _____

5. boring _____

6. to cheat or swindle _____

7. an area where goods are bought and sold

   _____

8. your view from a certain time or place

   _____

9. so excellent as to be set apart from others

   _____

10. a person who is easily taken advantage of

   _____

4 **Word Play**

Idioms

Write the vocabulary word that fits each idiom in the blanks below.

1. If you "stick out like a sore thumb," you are

   _____.

2. If something is "as plain as the nose on your face," it is

   _____.

3. If you "count your chickens before they're hatched," you could

   be making a wrong _____.

4. If you "stand in the way" of something, you

   _____ it.

5. If you're not "as deep as a well," you might be

   _____.

6. When someone "could be your double," it means they

   _____ you.

7. If you are "looking at this all wrong," you have a mistaken

   _____.

8. "If it were a snake it would have bit me" means that I did not

   _____ it.

9. If you "walk a mile in my shoes," then you will understand my

   _____.

10. If you listen "with an open mind" to an idea and then "jump

    on the band wagon," you are _____ to
    the new idea.

Vocabulary for the Senses

1 **Word Meanings**

Classifying

Vocabulary List

1. **bellow**
   (bel´ ō) v.
   to make a loud, deep sound

2. **coarse**
   (kors) adj.
   thick and rough

3. **din**
   (din) n.
   a loud, continuous noise

4. **grating**
   (grā´ ting) adj.
   making a harsh, irritating sound

5. **delectable**
   (di lek´ tə bəl) adj.
   very pleasing or delicious

6. **redolent**
   (red´ ə lənt) adj.
   giving off a pleasant odor

7. **scalding**
   (skôld´ ing) adj.
   almost boiling hot

8. **resounding**
   (ri zound´ ing) adj.
   full of loud, rich sound

9. **shrill**
   (shril) adj.
   sharp and high-pitched in sound

10. **tepid**
    (tep´ id) adj.
    slightly warm

 Write each word from the box under the heading of the sense you use to experience it. Use a dictionary if you need help.

attractive	delectable	redolent	sour
bellow	din	resounding	stench
bitter	grating	scalding	tangy
coarse	hazy	scented	tepid
dazzling	rank	shrill	velvety

Touch

_____

_____

_____

_____

Smell

_____

_____

_____

_____

Hearing

_____

_____

_____

_____

_____

Taste

_____

_____

_____

_____

Sight

_____

_____

_____

Score _____ (Top Score 20)

2 Reference Skills

Adjectives in Degrees

 Write the vocabulary words that fit with each group of adjectives.

1.
_____odorless_____
_____fragrant_____
_____smelly_____
_____rank_____
_____

2.
_____freezing_____
_____red-hot_____
_____chilly_____
_____
_____

3.
_____rough_____
_____smooth_____
_____silky_____
_____splintery_____
_____

4.
_____distasteful_____
_____yummy_____
_____horrible_____
_____bland_____
_____

• •

 Organize the adjectives from above in order of degree.

5.
| |
| |
| odorless |
| |
| fragrant |

6.
| freezing |
| |
| tepid |
| |
| red-hot |

7.
| splintery |
| |
| rough |
| smooth |
| |

8.
| |
| distasteful |
| |
| yummy |
| |

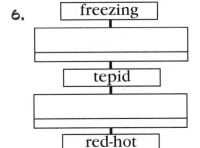

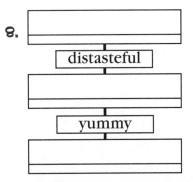

Vocabulary List

1. *bellow*

2. *coarse*

3. *din*

4. *grating*

5. *delectable*

6. *redolent*

7. *scalding*

8. *resounding*

9. *shrill*

10. *tepid*

3 Build New Vocabulary

Context Clues

Use context clues to replace the nonsense word with the appropriate vocabulary word in each sentence below. Write your answers in the blanks.

1. A kitchen in a medieval castle was a busy place, *wadadaling* with chopping and loud clashing noises.

   _____

2. Because of the great size of the kitchen, you could often hear the head cook *modabbo* orders to the other cooks from across

   the room. _____

3. The bustle began with the *timittle* sound of the rooster's

   morning cry. _____

4. The wheels of the food wagon made a loud *shracking* noise

   against the cobblestones. _____

5. Grains were ground into a rough, *rupishik* texture and stored

   in burlap sacks. _____

6. The cooks plunged the vegetables into huge kettles filled with

   yupperity water to cook. _____

7. The kitchen was *wowestza* with the wonderful smell of roasted

   meat. _____

8. It was an art to serve the food at a *zuraqua* temperature, not

   too hot or too cold. _____

4 Word Play

Alliteration and Assonance

 Fill in each blank with the vocabulary word that fits the alliteration or assonance in the sentence.

1. The _____ trill of the whippoorwill gives me chills.

2. The weight of the vibrating freight created an irritating

   _____.

3. A _____ within the inn begins in winter.

4. A _____ buffalo goes slowly to and fro in the snow.

5. We found the pounding sound was _____ all around.

6. The delicious dinner and _____ dessert made the Dad/Daughter Date delightful.

7. The horse pad was _____ and the source of much discourse, of course.

8. The _____ temperature was terrific for the tennis tournament.

• •

 ## Think About It

Alliteration and assonance are poetic tools that use sound for movement in your voice. It often helps to read poetry aloud so that you can hear the repeating consonants and vowels.

Vocabulary Review

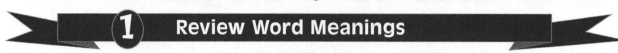

1 **Review Word Meanings**

Read the passage below. Then answer the questions about the boldfaced
vocabulary words.

The Legend of King Arthur

The legend of King Arthur originated in England in the Middle Ages and
has become one of the most **notable** stories in the English language. The
story began as the evil King Vortigern ordered the building of a strong
castle with a tower so high that nothing could **obstruct** his view of
approaching enemies. That very night, the castle was broken down.

Merlin, a man of great **perception**, gave King Vortigern **astonishing**
news: the dragons that fought nightly had created such a **din** that the walls
of the castle collapsed. Later that night, under the **luminous** moon, the
King hid himself so that he would not be **conspicuous**. Soon he heard
the **bellowing** of the dragons and saw their **coarse**, scaly skin. He saw
flames shoot from their mouths and felt the heat of their **scalding**
breath. Finally the white dragon defeated the red dragon.

Now read the following questions. Then
completely fill in the bubble of the
correct answer.

1. Which of the following is a definition of
   perception?
   Ⓐ cleverness
   Ⓑ awareness
   Ⓒ willingness to help

2. If something is *astonishing,* it is _____.
   Ⓐ ordinary
   Ⓑ clear
   Ⓒ amazing

3. Which of the following is a synonym of
   notable?
   Ⓐ outstanding
   Ⓑ average
   Ⓒ written

4. In which of the following sentences is
   din used in the correct context?
   Ⓐ The din coming from the kitchen made
     it hard for the knights to hear the king.
   Ⓑ The din coming from the kitchen
     smelled like roasting meat.
   Ⓒ The din coming from the kitchen had
     vegetables in it.

5. What word does not fit in the same
   category as the other two words?
   Ⓐ bellowing
   Ⓑ resounding
   Ⓒ scalding

6. What is a synonym of *coarse?*
   Ⓐ smooth
   Ⓑ rough
   Ⓒ even

② Review Word Meanings

Read the passage below. Then answer the questions about the boldfaced vocabulary words.

Merlin Explains the Battle of the Dragons

King Vortigern **recognized** that the battle of the dragons had some meaning that was not **obvious** to him. His **assumption** that Merlin could explain what it meant proved to be correct. "The red dragon represents you and all those who have **genetic** ties to you," Merlin said. "You brought **foreigners** to conquer the people, and you stole the throne of the rightful king. It is your **destiny** to be defeated by the two brothers who count the rightful king in their ancestry. The white dragon represents the two brothers who will regain the kingdom that is their **inheritance.** The people of this land shall give thanks for their **emancipation** from your evil rule. You will wander as a **nomad** without home or **citizenship** in any country. One of the brothers' descendants will become the greatest king who ever lived."

Now read the following questions. Then completely fill in the bubble of the correct answer.

1. Which of the following is of French origin and means "fate"?
   Ⓐ ancestry
   Ⓑ destiny
   Ⓒ emancipation

2. What is the base word of *assumptions?*
   Ⓐ assume
   Ⓑ assumpt
   Ⓒ belief

3. What word has a similar meaning to *conspicuous?*
   Ⓐ genetic
   Ⓑ recognized
   Ⓒ obvious

4. Which of the following sentences includes the correct definition of *nomad?*
   Ⓐ A nomad is a person who has no permanent home but wanders from place to place.
   Ⓑ A nomad is a person who never leaves his or her home.
   Ⓒ A nomad is a person who has many homes in different countries.

5. What word is an antonym of *emancipation?*
   Ⓐ freedom
   Ⓑ slavery
   Ⓒ proclamation

6. In which of the following sentences is *inheritance* used in the correct context?
   Ⓐ King Arthur's inheritance was to gather the best knights in the world at the Round Table.
   Ⓑ King Arthur's inheritance from his wife's father was the Round Table.
   Ⓒ King Arthur's inheritance was the knights of the Round Table.

7. Which of the following sets includes words that all relate to a person's family?
   Ⓐ emancipation, inheritance, foreigners
   Ⓑ ancestry, foreigners, destiny
   Ⓒ ancestry, genetic, descendants

8. Which of the following is a closed compound word?
   Ⓐ inheritance
   Ⓑ citizenship
   Ⓒ foreigners

③ Review Word Meanings

Read the passage below. Then answer the questions about the boldfaced vocabulary words.

Arthur Pulls the Sword from the Stone

True to Merlin's **foresight,** the two brothers, Aurelius and Uther, defeated King Vortigern. Uther became king, but when he died, the land was left without a king. All the lords and knights of Britain were **ambitious** to become king. They were **receptive** to Merlin's suggestion that they gather in the yard of a London church. It was there that the **virtuous** men of Britain saw a huge square stone with an **exceptional** sword stuck into it. On the sword was an **inscription** that read "Whoever shall pull this sword from the stone is born the rightful King of Britain."

Many lords and knights had **confidence,** but though they used their **utmost** strength, none could budge the sword from the stone. Months later, a **gracious** young fellow named Arthur volunteered to get the sword his foster brother had left at the inn. Finding the inn locked, Arthur thought he would borrow the sword in the stone. Young Arthur **resembled** a boy more than a man but was able to easily pull the sword from the stone.

....

Now read the following questions. Then completely fill in the bubble of the correct answer.

1. What word contains a prefix that means "out of" or "from"?
   Ⓐ resembled
   Ⓑ confidence
   Ⓒ exceptional

2. What word has the base word that means "writing"?
   Ⓐ exceptional
   Ⓑ inscription
   Ⓒ receptive

3. Which of the following is a definition of *utmost?*
   Ⓐ strongly desirous or eager
   Ⓑ almost all
   Ⓒ to the highest degree

4. Which of the following pairs of words mean the opposite of *virtuous?*
   Ⓐ evil, dishonest
   Ⓑ fair, good
   Ⓒ kind, courteous

5. In which of the following sentences is *resembled* used in the correct context?
   Ⓐ King Arthur resembled his knights at the Round Table every evening.
   Ⓑ King Arthur resembled the knights to tell about their adventures.
   Ⓒ King Arthur resembled his father.

6. A person who is *ambitious* to succeed has _____.
   Ⓐ a strong desire to succeed
   Ⓑ enough cleverness to succeed
   Ⓒ a small chance of succeeding

7. Which of the following are synonyms for *confidence?*
   Ⓐ faith in self
   Ⓑ assurance
   Ⓒ both a and b

8. Which of the following is a definition of *receptive?*
   Ⓐ having a strong desire
   Ⓑ open to new ideas
   Ⓒ unafraid of danger

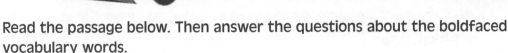

4 Review Word Meanings

Read the passage below. Then answer the questions about the boldfaced vocabulary words.

The Knights of the Round Table

Arthur was clearly the rightful king. He became known as a man of **integrity** and a **shrewd** ruler who was **evenhanded** with all of his people. The Knights would eat at the Round Table with King Arthur and Queen Guinevere and tell of their adventures in **exotic** lands. They had to speak over the **shrill** sound of cooks scolding their helpers and the **grating** of sharpening knives from the kitchen, which was **redolent** with the smell of roasting meat.

Of all the **exclusive** Round Table Knights, Sir Lancelot was the most notable for his bravery. He fought many battles, but he was such a skillful fighter that his few wounds were only **superficial.** The young King Arthur considered the Knights of the Round Table the best in the world, and his **outlook** on the future was very bright.

Now read the following questions. Then completely fill in the bubble of the correct answer.

1. Which of the following pairs are compound words?
   Ⓐ superficial, exotic
   Ⓑ outlook, evenhanded
   Ⓒ integrity, exclusive

2. What words are synonyms for *shrewd?*
   Ⓐ clever, practical, wise
   Ⓑ fair, just, honest
   Ⓒ gracious, charming, interesting

3. In which of the following sentences is *redolent* used in the correct context?
   Ⓐ The soup had been heated for so long that it was redolent.
   Ⓑ The soup was redolent with the smell of fresh vegetables.
   Ⓒ The soup tasted redolent to the hungry knights.

4. Which of the following is a definition for *exotic?*
   Ⓐ open to new ideas
   Ⓑ very loud and annoying
   Ⓒ strangely beautiful and unusual

5. In which of the following sets of words does *integrity* belong?
   Ⓐ gracious, virtuous, evenhanded
   Ⓑ outlook, perception, assumption
   Ⓒ exotic, ambitious, gracious

6. What word is an antonym of *superficial?*
   Ⓐ meaningless
   Ⓑ deep
   Ⓒ harmless

7. Which of the following is a definition of *evenhanded?*
   Ⓐ having good balance
   Ⓑ very skillful
   Ⓒ judging fairly

8. What word contains a prefix meaning "out of" or "from"?
   Ⓐ exclusive
   Ⓑ superficial
   Ⓒ integrity

Making a New Nation

1 Word Meanings

Completing Sentences

 Read each sentence below and write the vocabulary word that best fits.

1. Confederate
(kən fed′ ər it) *n.*
citizen or soldier of
the South in the
Civil War

2. invasion
(in vā′ zhən) *n.*
a forced entry

3. unity
(ū′ ni tē) *n.*
the state of being one

4. secede
(si sēd′) *v.*
to formally withdraw
from

5. battlefield
(bat′ əl fēld′) *n.*
place a battle
was fought

6. discharge
(dis′ chärj) *v.*
to shoot or send forth

7. cavalry
(kav′ əl rē) *n.*
soldiers who fight
on horseback

8. revolution
(rev′ ə loo′ shən) *n.*
overthrow of a
government

9. treaty
(trē′ tē) *n.*
a formal agreement
between nations

10. convention
(kən ven′ shən) *n.*
a formal meeting

1. Only 80 years after the American _____,
   the Civil War broke out between the northern states and the
   southern states.

2. When Abraham Lincoln was elected president, South Carolina

   called a state _____ in fear of losing their
   slaves.

3. The southern states announced that they would

   _____ from the Union.

4. The southern states named themselves the

   _____ States of America.

5. General Lee's first _____ of the North is
   known as the Battle of Antietam.

6. Thousands of soldiers on foot and in the

   _____ were killed.

7. The air will be filled with smoke when we

   _____ the rifles.

8. The Civil War did not end with a peace

   _____.

9. It would be many years before there was a true sense of

   _____ between the North and the South.

10. Lincoln delivered the Gettysburg Address on the site of the

    _____ in Gettysburg, Pennsylvania.

2 Reference Skills

Syllabication

 Use the dictionary to find each vocabulary word. Write each word and divide it into syllables using dots.

1. battlefield _____

2. cavalry _____

3. Confederate _____

4. discharge _____

5. opponent _____

6. invasion _____

7. revolution _____

8. secede _____

9. treaty _____

10. unity _____

• •

Match the vocabulary words below with their extended definitions.

11. _____ discharge   **A.** a place where a battle is or once was fought

12. _____ secede   **B.** to withdraw formally, often to form a new group

13. _____ Confederate   **C.** a military unit trained to fight on horseback

14. _____ convention   **D.** the entrance of an armed force

15. _____ revolution   **E.** to fire, shoot, or send forth

16. _____ battlefield   **F.** overthrow of the government by those governed

17. _____ invasion   **G.** a formal meeting for a special purpose

18. _____ treaty   **H.** the state or quality of being one

19. _____ cavalry   **I.** a formal agreement, especially between nations

20. _____ unity   **J.** a citizen of or someone who fought for the South in the Civil War

Vocabulary List

1. Confederate

2. invasion

3. unity

4. secede

5. battlefield

6. discharge

7. cavalry

8. revolution

9. treaty

10. convention

The Prefix *dis-*

 Write each word from the box below next to its definition. Use a dictionary if you need help.

disadvantage	discontinue	discourage
discredit	disgraceful	disfigure
disillusion	disloyal	disobedient
displeasure	discharge	disqualify
disunity	disown	discolor

1. to destroy belief in _____

2. something that interferes with success

   _____

3. the state of being annoyed _____

4. refusing to carry out orders _____

5. not faithful _____

6. to destroy the appearance of _____

7. to free from a false idea _____

8. shameful _____

9. to lessen the hope or confidence of _____

10. to stop _____

11. to remove from competition _____

12. to fire, send, or shoot forth _____

13. lack of togetherness _____

14. to refuse responsibility of _____

15. to change or spoil the color of _____

Word Play

Rhyming Poetry

Complete the rhyming poems below with Vocabulary List words.

Note to a Soldier in the Civil War

Take care that your weapon

does not _____
when you are riding on a barge.
The repercussions would be large.

Join Us

Will you join us in
Our institution?
We're fighting to win

A _____.

They Waged a War

The Confederate army waged
A war of promise, honor, and need
They swore on the freedom, that from the North

They were sure to _____.

Sweetie

The fighting has stopped
You've become such a sweetie
You've raised your white flag

And signed the club's _____.

• •

Earn two extra points for writing a poem of your own. Remember that it should include a vocabulary word.

_____

_____

_____

_____

1. **agenda**
(ə jen′ də) *n.*
a list of things to do

2. **segregation**
(seg′ ri gā′ shən) *n.*
separation of races

3. **intimidate**
(in tim′ i dāt′) *v.*
to influence by threats
or violence

4. **enforcement**
(en fors′ mənt) *n.*
act of making sure
that laws are obeyed

5. **act**
(akt) *n.*
something done;
a deed

6. **redeem**
(ri dēm′) *v.*
to regain or win back

7. **impose**
(im pōz′) *v.*
to burden someone

8. **interlude**
(in′ tər loōd′) *n.*
the time between
events

9. **district**
(dis′ trikt) *n.*
a division of a city,
state, or country

10. **carpetbagger**
(kär′ pit bag′ ər) *n.*
Northerner who went
to the South after the
Civil War

Reconstruction Vocabulary

1 **Word Meanings**

Classification

 Write the vocabulary word that best fits in each group of words.

outsider	separation	establish
Northerner	_____	force
_____	isolation	arrange
intruder	withdrawal	_____
urging		_____
compulsion		region
_____		area
coercion	**Reconstruction Era Words**	county
_____		list
motion		_____
deed		outline
accomplishment		plan
period	_____	regain
interval	frighten	compensate
space	threaten	_____
_____	scare	atone

② Reference Skills

Multiple Meanings

Read the dictionary entry for each word. Then complete each sentence below using one of the words. Write the number of the definition you use in the box after each sentence.

---

act *n.* **1.** something done; a deed: *Sometimes, telling the truth is an act of bravery.* **2.** the process of doing something: *My brother was caught in the act of eating the cookies.* **3.** a formal decision or law: *The legislature passed an act that reduces taxes.* **4.** one of the main divisions of a play: *We missed the first act of the play.*

impose *v.* **1.** to establish a duty by law: *The federal government has the right to impose taxes on its citizens.* **2.** to force: *The team members didn't appreciate his attempt to impose his will on them.*

redeem *v.* **1.** to regain or win back: *I will redeem my watch at the pawn shop.* **2.** to make up or compensate for: *I will try to redeem my rude behavior by apologizing.*

---

1. President Lincoln considered the South's attack on Fort Sumter

   to be an _____ of war. ☐

2. Although the Union was preserved, nothing could

   _____ the devastation and loss of 600,000

   lives caused by the Civil War. ☐

3. Some northern politicians wanted to

   _____ harsh penalties on the South after

   its defeat. ☐

4. It took many years for southern politicians to

   _____ the trust of the Northerners. ☐

5. Slavery was ended by an _____ of

   Congress in 1865. ☐

Vocabulary List

1. agenda
2. segregation
3. intimidate
4. enforcement
5. act
6. redeem
7. impose
8. interlude
9. district
10. carpetbagger

3 Build New Vocabulary

Colorful Compound Words

Write each compound word next to its definition. Use a dictionary if you need help.

cheapskate	shoo-in	mudslinger
laughingstock	carpetbagger	punch line
warmonger	skyrocket	has-been
hoodwink		

1. a Northerner who went to the South after the Civil War to take advantage of the disorganized situation

    _____

2. to trick _____

3. to rise suddenly and rapidly _____

4. a stingy person _____

5. a person who says offensive things about another, especially a political opponent _____

6. a person who will surely and easily be the winner of a contest

    _____

7. a person who tries to bring about political conflicts

    _____

8. the sentence that makes the point of a joke

    _____

9. a person who is no longer popular or successful

    _____

10. a person who is the object of ridicule

    _____

Word Play

Crossword Puzzle

 Solve the crossword puzzle clues using the Vocabulary List words.

ACROSS

1. to burden someone

2. a synonym for *frighten*

5. I need to stick to my _____ in order to get everything done today.

6. an antonym for *ignoring the law*

7. A good deed is a selfless _____.

8. an antonym of *integration*

9. a division of a city, state, or country

DOWN

1. a short period of time between events

3. Northerner who traveled south with intentions of taking a political or public position after the Civil War

4. a synonym for *regain* or *reclaim*

Vocabulary List

1. **elite**
   (i lēt´) *n.*
   the best or finest members

2. **integrate**
   (in´ ti grāt´) *v.*
   to bring together

3. **corporation**
   (kor´ pə rā´ shən) *n.*
   a group with legal power to act as one

4. **vertical**
   (vûr´ ti kəl) *adj.*
   upright

5. **compartment**
   (kəm pärt´ mənt) *n.*
   a division of an enclosed space

6. **department**
   (di pärt´ mənt) *n.*
   a division of an organization

7. **horizontal**
   (hor´ ə zon´ təl) *adj.*
   parallel to level ground

8. **structure**
   (struk´ chər) *n.*
   the way something is organized

9. **domain**
   (dō mān´) *n.*
   area owned or controlled

10. **linear**
    (lin´ ē ər) *adj.*
    relating to lines

Vocabulary for Organization

1 **Word Meanings**

Choosing the Best Word

 Write the vocabulary word that completes each sentence below.

1. Executives of a _____ have the right to enter into contracts.

2. Knowing the _____ of a company, or the way it is organized, will help you in working toward a promotion.

3. Each _____ has its own functions and responsibilities.

4. The executive offices are the official _____ of the people who make important decisions for the company.

5. Only the _____ and the most ambitious employees reach the highest positions in a large company.

6. The chain of command is usually _____, starting from the top and going downward.

7. Engineers _____ how things work with the elements of art in their design.

8. Design sketches of future products must be three-dimensional as well as _____.

9. The grid paper used for sketches has evenly spaced vertical and _____ lines.

10. A portfolio, which is a large case for carrying sketches, often has a separate _____ for pencils and other drawing instruments.

Reference Skills

Alphabetizing to the Second and Third Letters

 Write the words from the box below in alphabetical order.

compartment	corporation	equal
integrate	department	elite
collection	enclose	consider
delivery	chore	excess
domain	horizontal	duty

1. _____

2. _____

3. _____

4. _____

5. _____

6. _____

7. _____

8. _____

9. _____

10. _____

11. _____

12. _____

13. _____

14. _____

15. _____

Vocabulary List

1. elite
2. integrate
3. corporation
4. vertical
5. compartment
6. department
7. horizontal
8. structure
9. domain
10. linear

 3 **Build New Vocabulary**

The Base Word *part*

 Write each word from the box below next to its definition. Use a dictionary if you need help.

apartment	participate	participle
department	partition	particle
impart	compartment	particular
partial		

1. a set of rooms to live in _____

2. to tell or otherwise make known _____

3. a section of an enclosed space _____

4. distinct or apart from others _____

5. a division into distinct parts _____

6. not complete _____

7. a very small piece of something _____

8. to take part in _____

9. a verb form that sometimes functions as an adjective or a noun

    _____

10. a division of an organization _____

• •

Think About It

Knowing the meaning of a base word can help you decode an unfamiliar word. What other words can you think of that contain the base word *part?*

 **Word Play**

Rebus Equations

 Solve each rebus equation with vocabulary words.

1.  + po +  + tion =

_____

2.  +  =

_____

3. lin + 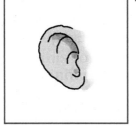 = _____

4. 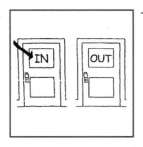 +  + grate =

_____

"Prefix Mix" Vocabulary

1 **Word Meanings**

Thinking Critically

Decide which sentence endings make sense and circle the correct letter or letters. Remember, there may be more than one correct answer.

1. subterranean
(sub′ tə rā′ nē ən) *adj.*
beneath the earth's
surface

2. supervisor
(soo′ pər vī′ zər) *n.*
one who oversees
with authority

3. transcontinental
(trans′ kon tə nen′ təl)
adj. going across a
continent

4. transfer
(trans′ fər) *v.*
to move from one
place to another

5. subside
(səb sīd′) *v.*
to lessen; to sink to
the bottom

6. supersede
(soo′ pər sēd′) *v.*
to take the place of

7. superhuman
(soo′ pər hū′ mən) *adj.*
far beyond normal
human ability

8. subordinate
(sə bor′ də nit) *adj.*
lower in rank

9. transition
(tran zish′ ən) *n.*
a change from one
form or stage to
another

10. submarine
(sub′ mə rēn′) *adj.*
beneath the surface
of the sea

1. If the new rule *supersedes* the old one, then
   a. the old rule is more important than the new one.
   b. the new rule replaces the old rule.

2. An example of a *transition* is
   a. getting used to attending a new school.
   b. sending an e-mail to a friend.

3. You can use the word *transcontinental* when talking about
   a. an airplane flight from New York to California.
   b. a railway system that crosses the United States.

4. It would be *superhuman* to
   a. read a story that is 100 pages long.
   b. lift a school bus with one finger.

5. An example of something that is *subterranean* is
   a. a subway that travels only underground.
   b. flood water that finally subsides.

6. You can be *subordinate* to
   a. a supervisor.
   b. a teacher.

7. An example of *submarine* life is
   a. a seagull that soars above the ocean.
   b. a school of fish.

8. An example of something you can *transfer* to a friend is
   a. a shopping mall.
   b. a package.

2 Reference Skills

Word Histories

 Read each word's history and write the vocabulary word that best matches.

1. from Latin *sub-* (under) + *terra* (earth)

   _____

2. from Medieval Latin *super-* (over) + *videre* (to see)

   _____

3. from Latin *sub-* (under) + *ordinare* (to arrange in order)

   _____

4. from Middle English *transferren,* from Old French *transferer,* from Latin *trans-* (across) + *ferre* (to bear)

   _____

• •

 Circle the letter of the definition that does NOT make sense based on the word histories shown above.

5. supervisor
   a. a person who ranks below others
   b. a person in charge of others
   c. a person who watches others performing on a job

6. transfer
   a. to bear, or carry, across
   b. to shift possession of a legal title from one person to another
   c. to cross the ocean

7. subterranean
   a. on the earth
   b. hidden or secret; under the surface
   c. below ground

8. subordinate
   a. below what can be seen
   b. not coming first in order
   c. in a position of lower rank

Vocabulary List

1. subterranean
2. supervisor
3. transcontinental
4. transfer
5. subside
6. supersede
7. superhuman
8. subordinate
9. transition
10. submarine

3 Build New Vocabulary

Synonyms

 Read the definition of each boldfaced word below. Then write the vocabulary word that is a synonym for the boldfaced word.

1. **supernatural:** existing outside the natural world; beyond what is natural or normal _____

2. **succeed:** to come next in time; to take an office or position to replace another _____

3. **subservient:** acting as a servant to others; subject to another's will _____

4. **abate:** to reduce in amount or degree _____

5. **phase:** a stage of development _____

6. **superintendent:** a person who manages an institution or a building _____

 Use the four vocabulary words you did not use above to complete each sentence below.

7. Jacques Cousteau was a scientist who explored the ocean, searching for new types of _____ life.

8. It is wise to _____ your money from a checking account to a savings account so that you are less likely to spend it.

9. Some buses are _____; you can ride them all the way from the Atlantic Ocean to the Pacific Ocean.

10. Molten lava is a _____ substance—at least until it erupts from a volcano!

4 Word Play

Visualization Strategy

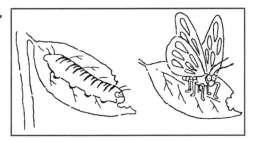 Study each picture. Write the vocabulary word from the box below that best matches the picture.

| superhuman | transition | supervisor |
| transcontinental | subterranean | |

1.

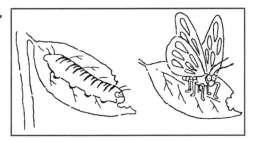

_____

2.

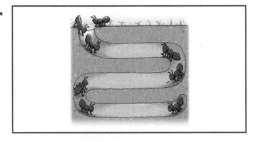

_____

3.

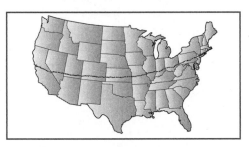

_____

4.

_____

5.

_____

Vocabulary List

1. **diagnosis**
(dī' əg nō' sis) *n.*
the process of
identifying a disease

2. **epidemic**
(ep' i dem' ik) *n.*
the rapid spread
of a disease

3. **immune**
(i mūn') *adj.*
protected from disease

4. **parasites**
(par' ə sīts') *n.*
organisms that live
on other organisms

5. **frail**
(frāl) *adj.*
lacking in strength

6. **anatomy**
(ə nat' ə mē) *n.*
the structure of
a living thing

7. **sterile**
(ster' əl) *adj.*
free from bacteria
and dirt

8. **vaccinate**
(vak' sə nāt') *v.*
to inject a disease
to build immunity

9. **diagrams**
(dī' ə gramz') *n.*
drawings that show
how things work

10. **nourishment**
(nûr' ish mənt) *n.*
something that
promotes health
and growth

Vocabulary for Health

1 Word Meanings

Cloze Sentences

 Write the vocabulary word that correctly completes each sentence below.

1. In the 1300s, a deadly _____ called the bubonic plague swept across Europe and killed millions of people.

2. The disease was spread by fleas, small _____ that lived on rats.

3. Even wealthy and well-educated people were not

_____ to the plague.

4. When a doctor made a _____ that a person had the plague, it was the same as a death sentence.

5. No medicines or _____ could help a person recover from the plague.

6. No one had discovered a way to _____ people so that they would be protected from ever getting the plague.

7. The first people in a household to die from the plague usually

were those who were elderly and _____.

8. In those days, doctors did not know they should make their

instruments _____ and kill the germs and bacteria on their hands.

9. Doctors of that time had little knowledge about human

_____ because it was against the law for them to study dead bodies.

10. There was very little medical information and few

_____ showing how the systems of the human body work.

2 · Reference Skills

Multiple Meanings

Read the dictionary entry for each word. Then complete each sentence below using one of the words. Write the number of the definition you use in the box after each sentence.

---

anatomy *n.* **1.** the branch of science that deals with the structure of animals: *Medical students must take courses in anatomy.* **2.** the structure of a body: *The anatomy of a fish is much different from that of a mammal.* **3.** a detailed examination or analysis: *The detective was methodical about reconstructing the anatomy of the crime.*

immune *adj.* **1.** protected from a disease naturally or by a vaccine: *Most people today are immune to the measles.* **2.** relating to antibodies, which are produced by the body in response to the presence of foreign substances: *The body has an immune reaction to diseases that it has been vaccinated against.* **3.** not affected by something: *Our teacher was immune to the noise of the train.*

sterile *adj.* **1.** not able to reproduce: *We found out that our cat is sterile.* **2.** not able to support the growth of plants: *The interior of the desert is sterile.* **3.** free of bacteria: *The nurse applied a sterile dressing to the wound.* **4.** having no imagination; stale: *The artist's work has become sterile.*

1. I am _____ to the teasing of my sister's

   friends. ☐

2. The instruments used for an operation must be

   _____. ☐

3. My doctor has a diagram of human _____

   in his office. ☐

4. The vaccine made the baby _____ to

   smallpox and polio. ☐

5. My skin has an _____ reaction to poison

   ivy. ☐

---

1. *diagnosis*

2. *epidemic*

3. *immune*

4. *parasites*

5. *frail*

6. *anatomy*

7. *sterile*

8. *vaccinate*

9. *diagrams*

10. *nourishment*

3 Build New Vocabulary

Context Clues

 Read each sentence. Use the context to figure out the meaning of the boldfaced word. Write the vocabulary word in the blank that is the synonym of each boldfaced word.

1. Foot-and-mouth disease is a highly contagious disease that affects farm animals such as cattle, pigs, sheep, and goats. This **pestilence** does not affect people, but people can spread it to

   healthy animals. _____

2. Animals affected by foot-and-mouth disease slobber more than usual, become uninterested in food, and have trouble walking because their feet have become **frangible.**

   _____

3. The United States has not had a case of foot-and-mouth disease since 1929. Americans who travel must be very careful when they return to the United States. They are not allowed to bring back **sustenance** from other countries, especially meat and dairy products. Officials at some airports have special dogs that smell luggage for signs of foreign food.

   _____

4. If people have been on a farm in another country, they must wash their clothing before entering the United States. They may be asked to dip their shoes in a solution that will kill any germs, clean off mud, and leave the shoes **aseptic.**

   _____

5. There is no way to vaccinate animals and make them **invulnerable** to this dangerous virus, so it is up to American citizens to help protect their country from foot-and-mouth

   disease. _____

Score _____ (Top Score 5)

Word Play

Examples

Write the vocabulary word next to its group of examples.

1. food, water, vitamins _____

2. leeches, ivy, bacteria _____

3. sketches, models, illustrations _____

4. sealed bandages, newly cleaned doctors' instruments

   _____

5. the plague, AIDS _____

6. a person who is ill, a person whose bones break easily

   _____

7. a doctor giving shots to a baby, to encourage immunity in a

   body _____

8. the structure of a horse's body, how a plant is put together

   _____

9. a doctor tells me I have chicken pox, the nurse decided I have

   an ear infection _____

10. protected from disease, not affected by contagious germs

   _____

Vocabulary Review

 **Review Word Meanings**

Read the passage below. Then answer the questions about the boldfaced vocabulary words.

The Civil War Begins

There was only an 80-year **interlude** between the American **Revolution** and the announcement by thirteen southern states that they would **secede** from the United States with hopes of their president **superseding** Abraham Lincoln. The leaders of these thirteen states, which were called the **Confederate** States of America, considered Abraham Lincoln to be their **opponent** rather than their president, and they felt that he was trying to **impose** his own **agenda** on them.

President Lincoln wanted to work with the Confederate leaders for the **preservation** of the **unity** of the United States, but they attacked a fort that was the **domain** of the federal government in Charleston, South Carolina. Although no one was killed, the **structure** of the fort was heavily damaged. The Civil War had begun.

Now read the following questions. Then completely fill in the bubble of the correct answer.

1. Which of the vocabulary words in the passage means "the time between events"?
   Ⓐ agenda
   Ⓑ revolution
   Ⓒ interlude

2. Which of the following means the same as "he was trying to impose his own agenda on them" in the passage above?
   Ⓐ he was trying to find out what they wanted to do
   Ⓑ he was trying to make them do what he wanted
   Ⓒ he was trying to make sure they were not late for meetings

3. Think critically and finish the sentence. If President Lincoln wanted to protect the unity of the United States, then he
   Ⓐ felt that the North and the South should divide into separate nations.
   Ⓑ believed that the North and the South should not be separated.
   Ⓒ did not care if the North and the South divided or stayed together.

4. Which vocabulary word fits in the classification *territory, property, area?*
   Ⓐ domain
   Ⓑ impose
   Ⓒ structure

5. Think critically and finish the sentence. If the Confederate states wanted their president to supersede President Lincoln, then they
   Ⓐ wanted their president to work under President Lincoln.
   Ⓑ wanted their president to take office after Lincoln's term.
   Ⓒ wanted their president to take President Lincoln's place.

2 Review Word Meanings

Read the passage below. Then answer the questions about the boldfaced vocabulary words.

The North Organizes Its Forces

The attack on Fort Sumter was an **act** of war against the Union that was against the laws of the United States. President Lincoln immediately asked for seventy-five thousand volunteers to join the U.S. **cavalry.** General Ulysses S. Grant soon won a major victory for the Union, and he became one of an **elite** group of generals who led the Union forces.

As the war went on, tens of thousands of soldiers marched in **linear** formation to meet on **battlefields** amid the **discharge** of guns and cannons. The War **Department** of the U.S. government was authorized to begin **enforcement** of the first draft, which required men between the ages of 20 and 46 to report for military duty. As historic **diagrams** show, the North controlled most of the factories, railroads, and supplies, and the Confederate position became unstable as there was no way to get supplies **transferred** to the South from other places.

Now read the following questions. Then completely fill in the bubble of the correct answer.

1. Which of the following divides *enforcement* into its correct syllables?
   - Ⓐ enforce•ment
   - Ⓑ en•for•ce•ment
   - Ⓒ en•force•ment

2. Which multiple meaning of *transfer* is used in the passage above?
   - Ⓐ to move or remove from one person or place to another
   - Ⓑ to give or sell the ownership of something
   - Ⓒ a ticket allowing a passenger to ride with no additional charge

3. Which list of vocabulary words is correctly alphabetized?
   - Ⓐ battlefields, cavalry, elite, department
   - Ⓑ act, discharge, department, enforcement
   - Ⓒ elite, enforcement, linear, transferred

4. Which of the following is the correct definition of *cavalry?*
   - Ⓐ division of the federal government
   - Ⓑ soldiers on horseback
   - Ⓒ a group of generals

5. Which of the following means the same as "tens of thousands of soldiers marched in *linear* formation" in the passage above?
   - Ⓐ tens of thousands of soldiers marched in a straight formation
   - Ⓑ tens of thousands of soldiers marched in backward formation
   - Ⓒ tens of thousands of soldiers marched in forward formation

6. Which list of words is alphabetized and divided into syllables correctly?
   - Ⓐ cav•al•ry, dis•charge, en•force•ment, e•lite
   - Ⓑ dis•ch•arge, e•lite, line•ar, trans•ferr•ed
   - Ⓒ de•part•ment, en•force•ment, lin•e•ar, trans•ferred

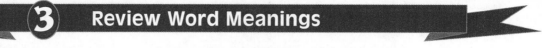

Read the passage below. Then answer the questions about the boldfaced vocabulary words.

The Human Losses of the Civil War

During the bloody Battle of Gettysburg, the North lost 23,000 men and the South lost 20,000. Many more lay wounded on the battlefield littered with pieces of cannonballs and clothing, and the lack of sanitary conditions in makeshift hospitals led to various **epidemics.**

Many of the soldiers were already **frail** from lack of **nourishment,** and they were no longer **immune** to the common infections that would normally **subside** after treatment. **Sterile** bandages and medicines that would prevent bacteria and other **parasites** from living on various parts of the soldiers' **anatomy** were in very short supply. There were not enough doctors to attend to those who were wounded or to make a **diagnosis** of diseases. The country would never be able to **redeem** the tremendous loss of life it suffered during the Civil War.

Now read the following questions. Then completely fill in the bubble of the correct answer.

1. The compound words *level off, melt away,* and *ease up* are synonyms for which vocabulary word?
   Ⓐ parasites
   Ⓑ frail
   Ⓒ subside

2. Which of the following means "the rapid spread of a disease"?
   Ⓐ parasites
   Ⓑ fragments
   Ⓒ epidemics

3. Which of the following is a definition of *frail?*
   Ⓐ relating to health and cleanliness
   Ⓑ weak and feeble
   Ⓒ protected from disease

4. In which of the following sentences is *redeem* used in the correct context?
   Ⓐ It took a long time for southern politicians to redeem the trust of Northerners.
   Ⓑ Doctors could not redeem many of the epidemics.
   Ⓒ Many soldiers were so frail that they could not redeem nourishment.

5. Which of the following means "the process of identifying a disease"?
   Ⓐ sanitary
   Ⓑ epidemic
   Ⓒ diagnosis

6. Which word with the base word *part* means "a division of an enclosed space"?
   Ⓐ department
   Ⓑ compartment
   Ⓒ impart

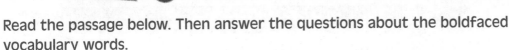

Read the passage below. Then answer the questions about the boldfaced vocabulary words.

The End of the Civil War

Almost two years after the Battle of Gettysburg, General Robert E. Lee, commander of the Confederate forces, requested a meeting with General Grant so that they could work out a peace **treaty.** Grant replied that he would accept only an unconditional surrender, which General Lee signed at the courthouse in the Virginia **district** of Appomattox.

The South was left in ruins. Its once-beautiful mansions, known for their graceful **vertical** pillars, had become run-down. Weeds and neglected animals had destroyed its fields of endless, **horizontal** rows of crops. Greedy **carpetbaggers** hoping to become rich filled the sleeping **compartments** of passenger trains from the North. When they arrived in the South, they set up dishonest **corporations** and tried to **intimidate** Southerners so that they could take advantage of them.

Although slavery had been abolished during the war, there was nothing stated in the law making it necessary to **integrate** blacks and whites. As a result, **segregation** between the races remained in the South for nearly 100 years after the Civil War because many people were not ready to make the **transition.**

....

Now read the following questions. Then completely fill in the bubble of the correct answer.

1. Which of the following words means "to influence by threats or violence"?
   Ⓐ intimidate
   Ⓑ integrate
   Ⓒ segregation

2. In which of the following sentences is *transition* used in the correct context?
   Ⓐ After the war, many people in the transition were happy.
   Ⓑ Some Southerners were not able to make the transition to a country without slavery.
   Ⓒ General Lee was forced to sign a transition.

3. Which vocabulary word best completes this sentence? The separation of the races, or _____, existed many years after the Civil War.
   Ⓐ corporations
   Ⓑ integration
   Ⓒ segregation

4. Which word is not a synonym for the vocabulary word *treaty?*
   Ⓐ agreement
   Ⓑ compact
   Ⓒ dessert

5. Into which category would *corporation* best fit?
   Ⓐ Northerners, traveled, scheming
   Ⓑ company, association, legal power
   Ⓒ runs side to side, level, with the horizon

Vocabulary List

1. **expedition**
(ek´ spə dish´ ən) *n.*
a journey made
for a purpose

2. **corral**
(kə ral´) *n.*
a fenced pen
for animals

3. **stampede**
(stam pēd´) *n.*
a rush of frightened
animals

4. **stake**
(stāk) *n.*
a sharp, pointed stick

5. **landowner**
(land´ ō´ nər) *n.*
person who owns
land

6. **boomtown**
(boom´ toun) *n.*
a rapidly growing
town

7. **vineyard**
(vin´ yərd) *n.*
grape garden

8. **sieve**
(siv) *n.*
a metal object with
holes for sifting

9. **forty-niner**
(for´ tē nī´ nər) *n.*
gold seeker in 1849

10. **deputy**
(dep´ yə tē) *n.*
one who is second in
charge

"Going West" Vocabulary

1 Word Meanings

Completing Sentences

 Write the correct vocabulary word in the blank for each sentence. Add *-s* to the word if necessary.

1. In 1842, the first American _____ into the Rocky Mountains was completed.

2. Three years later, 5,000 pioneers hoping to become _____ traveled westward.

3. It was common for the pioneers to see a buffalo _____.

4. In 1849, 80,000 _____ rushed to California hoping to find gold.

5. A miner who found a promising piece of land would pound a _____ into each corner to mark the boundaries.

6. A miner would scoop up the soil at the bottom of a stream with a _____ and then look closely for gold.

7. The quiet frontier town of San Francisco quickly became a _____ as thousands of people poured in.

8. The only law officers in a western frontier town were a sheriff and his _____.

9. Although many people went to California to mine for gold, others settled in the fertile valleys and planted _____.

10. Because horses were the only method of transportation, every farm and ranch had a _____.

② Reference Skills

Using Multiple References

Read the entries from the dictionary and the encyclopedia below. Then answer the questions that follow.

Dictionary

forty-niner (forʹ tē nīʹ nər) *n.* a person who went to California seeking gold in the gold rush of 1849.

Encyclopedia

forty-niner

article includes:
photograph
book reference
related article about John Sutter

two paragraphs of information about the forty-niners including facts. For example, *immigrants came from Europe, Asia, and South America. Mining camps with names like* Rough and Ready *were rough places to live. The forty-niners were also known as the Argonauts of '49.*

---

1. What reference source gives phonetic spellings for all

   entries? _____

2. What reference source gives a lot of information and details for a clearer understanding of what it meant to be a forty-niner?

   _____

3. Would the dictionary or the encyclopedia be the best place to find the part of speech of an entry word?

   _____

4. What entry would give you a short definition that would be

   easy to remember? _____

5. What entry gives other related sources to find out more about

   the subject? _____

6. Could you use a dictionary, an encyclopedia, or both to help you

   write a report on the forty-niners? _____

Vocabulary List

1. expedition
2. corral
3. stampede
4. stake
5. landowner
6. boomtown
7. vineyard
8. sieve
9. forty-niner
10. deputy

3 Build New Vocabulary

Context Clues

Read each sentence. Use context clues to help you match each underlined word with a definition from the box. Write the definition you choose in the blank.

Definitions

a source of great wealth

a natural piece of gold

tangy, uncooked bread

low hills at the base of mountains

a safe for valuables

person who looks for valuable materials

1. John Sutter's mill was located on the banks of the American River, in the rolling <u>foothills</u> of the Sierra Nevada mountains.

_____

2. Thousands of <u>prospectors</u> sifted the water of the river in search of gold.

_____

3. Some lucky miners found large chunks of gold, whereas others found only a few <u>nuggets</u>.

_____

4. The Wells Fargo Company would buy gold from the miners or store it for them in a <u>strongbox</u>.

_____

5. A San Francisco bakery became known for the <u>sourdough</u> that it used in making bread to supply the miners.

_____

6. By the late 1850s, California was no longer a <u>bonanza</u> for gold seekers. In 1897, a new gold rush began in Alaska.

_____

 **Word Play**

Idioms

 Each of the following idioms came into use in the Old West. Write the definition from the box that best matches each boldfaced idiom in the blanks below.

Definitions	
make a lot of money	suddenly
wait a minute	move away
endure hardship or pain	work out
get even	leader

1. My idea for a new business didn't **pan out.**

   _____

2. Kevin thinks he tricked me, but I'll **fix his wagon!**

   _____

3. **Hold your horses!** You can't leave the table until you finish your peas.

   _____

4. Let's **pull our stakes** and move to New York.

   _____

5. You're going to have to **bite the bullet** and admit to making a

   mistake. _____

6. He's going to **strike it rich** someday.

   _____

7. She's a real **trailblazer.**

   _____

8. I decided to go **on the spur of the moment.**

   _____

1. **cog**
   (kog) *n.*
   tooth on a gear

2. **pulley**
   (pŏŏl´ ē) *n.*
   moveable wheel
   in a machine

3. **gear**
   (gir) *n.*
   toothed wheel
   in a machine

4. **valve**
   (valv) *n.*
   device that controls
   the flow of liquid

5. **current**
   (kûr´ ənt) *n.*
   flow of electricity

6. **generator**
   (jen´ ə rā tər) *n.*
   a machine that
   makes energy

7. **appliance**
   (ə plī´ əns) *n.*
   a household machine

8. **lever**
   (lev´ ər) *n.*
   a bar for lifting

9. **gauge**
   (gāj) *n.*
   measuring tool

10. **diesel**
    (dē´ zəl) *n.*
    an air-compression
    engine

Machines and Tools

(1) **Word Meanings**

Word Relationships

For each of the following word sets, circle the word that is not related to the other two.

1. handle	motor	generator
2. liquid	cog	gear
3. gasoline	diesel	measure
4. gear	liquid	wheel
5. appliance	refrigerator	lever
6. wheel	gasoline	pulley
7. lever	wheel	bar
8. gauge	measure	pulley
9. cog	current	appliance
10. lever	generator	pulley

 Think About It

Knowing how words relate to each other can help you organize them in your mind. Can you think of more words that relate to this week's Vocabulary List words?

② Reference Skills

Multiple Meanings

 Read the dictionary entry for each word. Then complete each sentence below using one of the words. Write the number of the definition that you used on the blank after each sentence.

---

current *n.* **1.** air or water that is continuously flowing along the same path: *The heater provided a warm current of air.* **2.** the flow of electricity in a circuit: *A switch turns the current on and off. adj.* **3.** belonging to the present time: *I did better on my current math test than I did on the one before.*

gauge *n.* **1.** an instrument used for measuring: *I used a gauge to check the air pressure of the tire.* **2.** a means of judging, a standard: *The amount of money a person makes is not necessarily a gauge of success.* **3.** thickness or diameter, as of a wire: *The gauge of the wire is 4 millimeters.*

gear *n.* **1.** a wheel with a toothed edge that fits into the teeth of another wheel: *The chain on my bicycle came off the large gear.* **2.** an arrangement of such wheels used for changing movements: *My father put his truck in low gear to climb the hill.* **3.** equipment used for a specific purpose: *I packed my camping gear in the car. v.* **4.** to change something to make it suit something else: *When we go hiking, we have to gear our speed to my little sister's speed.*

---

1. Some cars have a stick shift to change from one

   _____ to another. _____

2. My math test scores are a good _____ of

   how well I am doing in math. _____

3. I write in my journal every day to keep it

   _____. _____

4. Some watches have tiny _____ to make

   the hands move in a circle. _____

5. The _____ of the Mississippi River is

   very strong in some places. _____

Machines and Tools • Reference Skills   Score _____ (Top Score 10)   Unit 5 • Lesson 26   **103**

Vocabulary List

1. cog
2. pulley
3. gear
4. valve
5. current
6. generator
7. appliance
8. lever
9. gauge
10. diesel

3 Build New Vocabulary

The Greek Root *gen* and Latin Word *currere*

Use context clues in the sentences to help you figure out the meaning of the underlined word. Write the letter of the definition in the blank beside the sentence.

a. not concerned with details or specifics
b. mild-mannered
c. a highly skilled or intelligent person
d. flowing writing that connects the letters of a word
e. having a willingness to give freely
f. a small section of a chromosome that determines a trait of an individual
g. real paper money that is used by being passed around
h. a group of individuals born at about the same time
i. being what it seems to be; real
j. a moveable arrow on a computer screen

1. I learned to write in <u>cursive</u> in the third grade. _____

2. Wolfgang Amadeus Mozart was a musical <u>genius</u>. _____

3. The Baby Boomer <u>generation</u> came after World War II. _____

4. I didn't understand all the signs, but I got the <u>general</u> idea of what the sign language interpreter meant. _____

5. Is this dollar bill <u>genuine</u> or fake? _____

6. The mouse moves the <u>cursor</u> around on the computer screen. _____

7. None of us got my mother's <u>gene</u> for blue eyes. _____

8. Mother Teresa was very <u>generous</u> with her time and energy as she helped the poor in India. _____

9. Some <u>currency</u> is used so much that it wears out. _____

10. Large draft horses are usually very <u>gentle</u>. _____

 **Word Play**

Finding and Defining

 Find and circle all ten vocabulary words. There are two hidden mystery words. Can you find them?

X	A	G	A	M	P	N	E	V	L	A	V	J	A
E	I	J	O	K	T	U	M	S	E	C	R	P	S
D	Y	B	L	C	Z	A	Q	W	S	I	P	V	E
G	E	N	E	R	A	T	O	R	E	L	C	S	N
B	L	E	V	S	Z	P	U	L	I	Y	U	L	I
K	L	V	E	R	D	G	H	A	D	F	G	O	H
E	U	S	R	M	U	X	N	U	A	R	R	O	C
E	P	L	M	A	B	C	U	R	R	E	N	T	A
R	I	H	U	H	E	H	J	M	T	U	Q	O	M
F	T	E	G	U	A	G	A	E	R	S	P	P	A

• •

 Match the following vocabulary words with their definitions.

11. _____ diesel

12. _____ valve

13. _____ gear

14. _____ appliance

15. _____ generator

A. a machine that changes mechanical energy into electrical energy

B. an engine that uses compressed air to heat and ignite fuel

C. a device used to control the flow of liquids or gases

D. machine for household use

E. a toothed wheel shaped to fit similar wheels in a machine

1. export
(ek sport´) *v.*
to send out of
a country

2. inventory
(in´ vən tor´ ē) *n.*
a list of goods in stock

3. transaction
(tran sak´ shən) *n.*
a business deal

4. budget
(buj´ it) *n.*
a plan for spending

5. import
(im port´) *v.*
to bring goods
into a country

6. enterprise
(en´ tər prīz´) *n.*
an important or
difficult financial
project

7. proceeds
(prō´ sēdz) *n.*
money made

8. financial
(fi nan´ shəl) *adj.*
related to money

9. commodity
(kə mod´ i tē) *n.*
goods bought
and sold

10. executive
(eg zek´ yə tiv) *n.*
person in charge
of a business

Economy Vocabulary
1 Word Meanings
Definition Sentences

 Write *T* in the blank if the definition sentence for the vocabulary word is correct. Write *F* if the sentence is false. For every *F* answer, write the vocabulary word that fits the definitions.

1. To *import* is to send goods into a foreign country. _____

_____

2. *Financial* is an adjective relating to money. _____

_____

3. An *executive* is a business deal. _____

_____

4. A *commodity* is a list of goods that are in stock. _____

_____

5. A *commodity* is something that could be on a list to be bought

and sold. _____ _____

6. To *import* is to ship goods into a country from a foreign

country. _____ _____

7. A *proceed* is a plan for spending. _____

_____

8. An *executive* is a person who makes decisions for a business.

_____ _____

9. *Enterprise* is money made from a business or profit. _____

_____

10. A *transaction* is a business organization. _____

_____

② Reference Skills

Guide Words

 Compare each vocabulary word with the guide words beside it. Decide where the vocabulary word would be located in a dictionary and circle *before*, *after*, or *on this page*.

Vocabulary Words	Guide Words			
1. budget	buckle/buffalo	before	after	on this page
2. commodity	common/communicate	before	after	on this page
3. enterprise	entertain/entrance	before	after	on this page
4. executive	exchange/excuse	before	after	on this page
5. export	explain/expose	before	after	on this page
6. financial	finch/finish	before	after	on this page
7. import	impinge/impossible	before	after	on this page
8. inventory	introduce/invent	before	after	on this page
9. proceeds	probability/procedure	before	after	on this page
10. transaction	tranquil/transcript	before	after	on this page

• •

 Match the vocabulary words with their definitions.

11. _____ import   **A.** a business deal

12. _____ enterprise   **B.** person in charge of a business

13. _____ executive   **C.** a plan for spending

14. _____ export   **D.** a financial undertaking

15. _____ budget   **E.** good bought and sold

16. _____ financial   **F.** to bring good into a country

17. _____ transaction   **G.** related to money

18. _____ commodity   **H.** to send out of a country

Vocabulary List

1. export
2. inventory
3. transaction
4. budget
5. import
6. enterprise
7. proceeds
8. financial
9. commodity
10. executive

3 Build New Vocabulary

The Prefix *trans-*

 Read the words in the box and their definitions. Write the words in the blanks in the sentences below. Remember that the prefix *trans-* means "across."

transcontinental: across a continent	**translate:** to change into another language
transcript: a written record	**transmit:** to send
transfer: to move from one place to another	**transplant:** to uproot and plant in another place
transfigure: to change the appearance of	**transport:** to carry from one place to another
transit: the act of traveling through	**transpose:** to reverse the order of

1. Trains are used to _____ coal.

2. Spring is the best time to _____ flowers.

3. The construction of the first _____ railway in North America began during the Civil War.

4. Radios _____ electromagnetic waves.

5. A coat of paint can _____ a dull room into a bright one.

6. To _____ a word is to spell it backwards.

7. A court reporter writes a _____ of every word that is spoken in court.

8. Canadian geese are in _____ when they fly south for the winter.

9. You can have someone _____ a foreign language for you.

10. It can be difficult to _____ to a new school in the middle of the year.

4   Word Play

Riddles

Write the vocabulary word that solves each riddle below. Use the underlined clues to help you choose the right word.

1. They might not reach perfection, but workers can <u>expect</u> direction from these. _____

2. This is what a business <u>action</u> is called.

   _____

3. It's <u>commonly</u> traded for money. _____

4. A firm one of these does not <u>budge</u> even for something that you really want to buy. _____

5. You might <u>proceed</u> to split these with your partners.

   _____

6. It's a fantastic feeling when I <u>finally finish figuring</u> out these <u>matters</u>. _____

7. You won't have to <u>invent</u> an answer to what is in the store if you have one of these. _____

8. It <u>exits</u> from our <u>port</u>. _____

9. The goods brought into our country are <u>import</u>ant to our economic system. _____

10. If you <u>enter</u> into this, you become part of a difficult or important financial project. _____

Economy Vocabulary • Word Play   Score _____ (Top Score 10)   Unit 5 • Lesson 27   **109**

Vocabulary List

1. **navigation**
   (nav´ i gā´ shən) *n.*
   act of guiding a ship
   or aircraft

2. **vessel**
   (ves´ əl) *n.*
   a large boat

3. **cargo**
   (kär´ gō) *n.*
   goods carried by
   a ship

4. **galley**
   (gal´ ē) *n.*
   a kitchen in a ship
   or airplane

5. **yacht**
   (yot) *n.*
   pleasure boat

6. **rigging**
   (rig´ ing) *n.*
   ropes that support
   sails on a ship

7. **armada**
   (är mä´ də) *n.*
   fleet of warships

8. **clipper**
   (klip´ ər) *n.*
   fast-sailing cargo ship

9. **shipshape**
   (ship´ shāp´) *adj.*
   in good order

10. **contraband**
    (kon´ trə band´) *n.*
    goods shipped
    against the law

Ships and Sailing

1 Word Meanings

Examples

 Write the vocabulary words that correctly answer each question below.

1. What three vocabulary words name a single ship?

   _____ _____

   _____

2. What vocabulary word names a group of ships?

   _____

3. What two vocabulary words name something that is a part of a

   ship? _____

   _____

4. What two vocabulary words name something that can be

   carried in a ship? _____

   _____

5. What vocabulary word describes the state of order on a ship?

   _____

6. Which vocabulary word describes the main duty of the captain

   of a ship? _____

• •

Think About It

Connecting words and their definitions with examples that you
have seen or experienced will make these words more usable
and memorable in the process of building your vocabulary skills.

② Reference Skills

Phonetic Spelling in Context

Read the questions and answers aloud. Fill in the blanks in the answers with the appropriate vocabulary words that are phonetically spelled in the questions.

Q. How do sailors control the (nav′ i gā′ shən) of large (klip′ ər) ships?

A. The _____ of a _____ ship is controlled by moving the rudder and by pulling or releasing the ropes that support the sails—this is called rigging.

Q. Why was the English (ves′ əl) superior to that of the Spanish in their famous (är mä′ də)?

A. The English _____ was believed to be smaller and quicker, but it was actually larger with stronger cannons than a

ship in the Spanish _____.

Q. What is the difference between (kon′ trə band′) and (kär′ gō)?

A. _____ is actually an illegal form of

_____, or goods carried on a ship.

Q. Did his (yot) have a (gal′ ē)?

A. His _____ had a beautiful

_____ with all the conveniences of home. It was fully stocked with fresh food and was clean, neat, and in shipshape order for his guests.

Vocabulary List

1. navigation

2. vessel

3. cargo

4. galley

5. yacht

6. rigging

7. armada

8. clipper

9. shipshape

10. contraband

3 Build New Vocabulary

Words of Spanish Origin

 Match each word of Spanish origin with its definition. Use a dictionary if you need help.

1. _____ apricot

2. _____ barbecue

3. _____ barricade

4. _____ cocoa

5. _____ cork

6. _____ armada

7. _____ galleon

8. _____ hammock

9. _____ poncho

10. _____ puma

11. _____ vanilla

12. _____ cargo

A. a cape with a hole that is slipped over the head

B. a quickly-made barrier used to stop an enemy

C. a mountain lion

D. a fleet of warships

E. a light, sweet flavoring used in food

F. an orange-colored fruit that looks like a small peach

G. goods carried by a ship

H. meat is roasted over an open fire outdoors

I. a light, thick tree bark used chiefly as stoppers for bottles

J. a sailing ship used between the fifteenth and seventeenth centuries

K. a swing bed that is hung between two trees or poles

L. a brown powder made from cacao seeds and used in making chocolate

4 Word Play

Analogies

 Complete each analogy with a vocabulary word.

1. **cargo** is to **legal** as

   _____ is to **illegal**

2. **armada** is to **war** as

   _____ is to **pleasure**

3. **messy** is to **disorder** as

   _____ is to **order**

4. **drive** is to **car** as

   _____ is to **ship**

5. **vehicle** is to **road** as

   _____ is to **water**

6. **sleeping** is to **bedroom** as

   cooking is to _____

7. **reins** are to **horseback riding** as

   _____ is to **sailing**

8. **bus** is to **passengers** as

   ship is to _____

9. **fleet** is to **English** as

   _____ is to **Spanish**

10. **jet** is to **aircraft** as

    _____ is to **ship**

Vocabulary List

1. **flurry**
(flûr´ ē) *n.*
a short, light snowfall

2. **typhoon**
(tī foon´) *n.*
hurricane

3. **blizzard**
(bliz´ ərd) *n.*
a blowing snowstorm

4. **precipitation**
(pri sip´ i tā´ shən) *n.*
rain, snow, hail

5. **frigid**
(frij´ id) *adj.*
freezing cold

6. **arid**
(ar´ id) *adj.*
dry

7. **thermostat**
(thûr´ mə stat´) *n.*
an instrument that
controls temperature

8. **sweltering**
(swel´ tər ing) *adj.*
very hot

9. **drought**
(drout) *n.*
a long period
of no rain

10. **front**
(frunt) *n.*
border of two
air masses

Weather Vocabulary

1 **Word Meanings**

Word Relationships

 Circle the letter for each correct answer. (**Hint:** There is
more than one correct answer for each item.)

1. The relationships between *frigid* and *sweltering* are that both
   a. mean "freezing."
   b. are extremes in temperature.
   c. are opposites.
   d. are synonyms.

2. The relationships between a *typhoon* and a *blizzard* are that both
   a. are severe storms.
   b. have freezing temperatures.
   c. produce large amounts of precipitation.
   d. come after a period of flurries.

3. The relationships between *arid* and *drought* are that
   a. both occur only in deserts.
   b. both are associated with a lack of rain.
   c. few plants can survive in either condition.
   d. both occur along the boundary of a front.

4. The relationships between *front* and *precipitation* are that
   a. precipitation usually occurs along the boundaries of a front.
   b. a front usually prevents precipitation.
   c. a front can carry precipitation with it as it moves.
   d. precipitation is always frigid with a front.

5. The relationships between *flurry* and *precipitation* are that
   a. a flurry is not precipitation.
   b. a flurry is one kind of precipitation.
   c. all precipitation comes in a flurry.
   d. a short, light, freezing precipitation is called a flurry.

② Reference Skills

Atlases and Almanacs

Read the following information from the atlas and almanac. Use the information to answer the questions about the vocabulary words. Write the letter of the correct answer in the blank.

A hurricane is a storm with winds rotating counterclockwise over tropical ocean waters. It has precipitation and winds that travel 73 miles per hour or more. In the western Pacific, these storms are known as typhoons.

"Mount Waialeale, Hawaii, is the rainiest place in the world. It has an average annual rainfall of 460 inches."

Lowest Average Annual Precipitation: Arica, Chile, South America receives 0.03 inches.

Arica, Chile, is located in an area where the land is not used for farming or ranching.

Mount Waialeale, Hawaii, is located in a tropical rain forest.

1. _____ What is true about *typhoons?*
   a. They are storms over the Pacific Ocean.
   b. They have winds less than 73 miles per hour.
   c. a and b

2. _____ What is true about Arica, Chile?
   a. The people farm the land because of the amount of precipitation.
   b. It is too arid to farm or ranch.
   c. It snows a lot there.

3. _____ What is true about *precipitation?*
   a. A rain forest can have 460 inches of rain per year.
   b. Farming depends on precipitation.
   c. a and b

4. _____ What is true about almanacs and atlases?
   a. They can help you understand more about the meanings of words.
   b. They are a good source of information for school reports.
   c. a and b

Vocabulary List

1. *flurry*
2. *typhoon*
3. *blizzard*
4. *precipitation*
5. *frigid*
6. *arid*
7. *thermostat*
8. *sweltering*
9. *drought*
10. *front*

3 Build New Vocabulary

Sorting Synonyms

Each word in the box is a synonym of *frigid*, *sweltering*, *arid*, or *precipitation*. Write each word under its correct synonym heading. Use a dictionary or thesaurus if you need help.

biting	flurry	simmering
bitter	freezing	sleet
blazing	glacial	smoldering
bone-dry	hail	snow
broiling	parched	stifling
dry	piercing	thirsty
dusty	rain	waterless
fiery	shower	wintry

Frigid	**Arid**	**Sweltering**	**Precipitation**
_____	_____	_____	_____
_____	_____	_____	_____
_____	_____	_____	_____
_____	_____	_____	_____
_____	_____	_____	_____
_____	_____	_____	_____

Word Play

All in a Word

Identify the vocabulary word from which the following words can be made. Each sentence will give you a clue.

1. **dog, hut, tough** (We are hoping for rain, but haven't seen any in a long time.) _____

2. **tear, patient, paint** (The clouds are full and the weather is humid; soon we will see this.) _____

3. **not, hoot, toy** (You might see one of these if you are near the western Pacific Ocean in the months of July, August, September or October.) _____

4. **wet, ring, tinge** (The thermometer reads 110 degrees Fahrenheit, and not one cloud is in the sky.)

_____

5. **grid, rid, fig** (She forgot her winter jacket on the coldest day this year; this is how she felt.) _____

 Circle the letter of each word that could be formed using the letters of the vocabulary word given. (**Hint:** More than one answer might be correct.)

6. **arid**
   a. are   **b.** rid   **c.** dare

7. **blizzard**
   a. lizard   **b.** blind   **c.** bid

8. **flurry**
   a. four   **b.** furry   **c.** rule

9. **thermostat**
   a. some   **b.** more   **c.** storm

10. **front**
   a. nor   **b.** ton   **c.** torn

Vocabulary Review

1 Review Word Meanings

Read the passage below. Then answer the questions about the boldfaced vocabulary words.

Going West

In 1849, tens of thousands of **forty-niners** headed to California on an **expedition** to search for gold. Some traveled across the country on trails and encountered herds of buffalo searching for water during the summer **drought.** The travelers were careful not to startle the buffalo because they could have been easily trampled in a **stampede.** They suffered from **sweltering** heat as they crossed the **arid** deserts of the Southwest.

Other forty-niners crossed the Rocky Mountains, where they often encountered a scattered **flurry** of snow. Heavier **precipitation** would follow when a cold **front** met a warm front, sometimes creating a full-fledged **blizzard.** These travelers had to suffer **frigid** temperatures during these severe winter storms.

Now read the following questions. Then completely fill in the bubble of the correct answer.

1. What sentence correctly states the relationship between a *flurry* and a *blizzard?*
   Ⓐ Both occur during sweltering temperatures.
   Ⓑ Both are forms of precipitation.
   Ⓒ Both are a type of front.

2. In which sentence is *expedition* used correctly?
   Ⓐ President Jefferson sent Lewis and Clark to make an expedition into the western frontier.
   Ⓑ President Jefferson formed an expedition to decide who should explore the western frontier.
   Ⓒ Lewis and Clark gave President Jefferson an expedition of their journey.

3. Which of the following is a definition of *stampede?*
   Ⓐ an enclosed pen in which animals are kept
   Ⓑ a rush of frightened animals
   Ⓒ a herd of animals gathered together for protection

4. Which one is NOT an example of a *forty-niner?*
   Ⓐ someone who came to California for the Gold Rush
   Ⓑ someone who searched for gold in the West in 1849
   Ⓒ someone who is 49 years old

5. What is the relationship between *front* and *drought?*
   Ⓐ A front causes a drought.
   Ⓑ A front can bring rain to stop the drought.
   Ⓒ A drought is a type of front.

② Review Word Meanings

Read the passage below. Then answer the questions about the boldfaced vocabulary words.

More Arrivals in California

Some forty-niners reached California by sailing on **clippers** across the Gulf of Mexico to Panama. There they crossed the thin strip of land to the Pacific Ocean and boarded other **vessels** bound for San Francisco. The more comfortable vessels were in **shipshape** order and provided the passengers with food prepared in the **galley.** Ten thousand Australians also sailed to California in 1849, hoping that they would not encounter any **typhoons** or unfriendly ships transporting **contraband.**

With the arrival of so many people in California, it became necessary to **import** shiploads of food and supplies. With so many ships carrying passengers and **cargo,** the San Francisco Harbor looked like it was filled with the sails and **riggings** of a huge **armada.**

Now read the following questions. Then completely fill in the bubble of the correct answer.

1. Which of the following pairs names parts of a ship?
   Ⓐ cargo, appliances
   Ⓑ vessels, contraband
   Ⓒ galley, riggings

2. What is the Spanish word meaning "a fleet of ships"?
   Ⓐ vessels
   Ⓑ yachts
   Ⓒ armada

3. Which of the following is a correct definition of *contraband?*
   Ⓐ goods being transported illegally
   Ⓑ goods being carried by a ship
   Ⓒ goods being brought into a country

4. If something is *shipshape,* it is _____.
   Ⓐ neat and organized
   Ⓑ able to float on water
   Ⓒ shaped like a ship

5. In which sentence is *clippers* used correctly?
   Ⓐ The captain clippers the ship carefully into the harbor.
   Ⓑ Clippers were the fastest ships.
   Ⓒ The clippers were so quick and clever, they could steal a fish from a fishing line.

6. Which of the following mutiple meanings for the *vessel* is used in the passage above?
   Ⓐ a tube that carries bodily fluid, such as in a vein or an artery
   Ⓑ a hollow container, as for liquids
   Ⓒ a ship or large boat

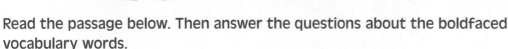

Review Word Meanings

Read the passage below. Then answer the questions about the boldfaced vocabulary words.

The Prospectors

Prospectors loaded supplies in San Francisco, led their horses from the **corral,** and began their search for gold, Earth's most precious **commodity.** They pounded **stakes** into the ground to mark the land they were claiming. Then prospectors began sifting the dirt from the bottom of the stream with a **sieve.**

Henry Wells and William Fargo decided to invest their money in an **enterprise** that provided **financial** and mail services for the prospectors. The two **executives** set up stations where miners could collect mail and make banking **transactions.** Soon the growing Wells Fargo Company was able to use its **proceeds** to buy thirty coaches to transport passengers and mail from St. Louis to California.

Now read the following questions. Then completely fill in the bubble of the correct answer.

1. Which of the following contains a Latin prefix that means "across"?
   Ⓐ invest
   Ⓑ proceeds
   Ⓒ transaction

2. Which of the following is a definition of *enterprise?*
   Ⓐ a financial project
   Ⓑ the proceeds of a company
   Ⓒ the person in charge of a company

3. Which of the following is an adjective that means "relating to money"?
   Ⓐ commodity
   Ⓑ enterprise
   Ⓒ financial

4. In which of the following sentences is *commodity* used correctly?
   Ⓐ The executives of the commodity started a new company.
   Ⓑ The executives made a commodity with a bank.
   Ⓒ The executives decided that gold was the commodity that they would invest in.

5. Which of the following relationships is NOT possible?
   Ⓐ to invest money in an enterprise
   Ⓑ to invest executives in a transaction
   Ⓒ to invest proceeds in a commodity

6. Which of the following is a list of synonyms for *enterprise?*
   Ⓐ come into, arrive, join, pass through
   Ⓑ amuse, excite, host, charm
   Ⓒ undertaking, venture, project, task

Review Word Meanings

Read the passage below. Then answer the questions about the boldfaced vocabulary words.

New Transportation to and in California

The gold rush quickly transformed San Francisco from a small frontier town with only a sheriff and a **deputy** to a bustling **boomtown.** Congress passed a bill in 1862 that provided money to connect the eastern railroads to Californian railroads. More than 1,776 miles of track were laid without the use of modern digging tools or **gauges.** By 1869, San Francisco was filled with the sound of steam engines. Because they were powered by steam being forced through **valves,** they were much noisier than modern **diesel** engines.

The first streetcars powered by electric **current** began operation in San Francisco in 1873. The cars were connected to an underground wire cable that had **pulleys** at each end. These cable cars were controlled by **levers.** At the end of the levers were several **gears** with **cogs** that fit together when the operator engaged the gears.

Now read the following questions. Then completely fill in the bubble of the correct answer.

1. What are two correct definitions for *current*?
   Ⓐ at the present time, the flow of electricity
   Ⓑ at the present time, an instrument used for measuring
   Ⓒ in the future, a device that controls the flow of liquid

2. Which of the following sets contains words that name machine parts?
   Ⓐ pulley, lever, gear
   Ⓑ valve, cog, gauge
   Ⓒ both A and B

3. Which word means "a means of judging" and "a measuring tool"?
   Ⓐ valve
   Ⓑ diesel
   Ⓒ gauge

4. If a town is a *boomtown,* it _____.
   Ⓐ is deserted because most residents have moved away
   Ⓑ is growing very quickly
   Ⓒ is the capital city of a state

5. Which of the following sentences uses *gear* in the correct context?
   Ⓐ Prospectors packed their gear on horses and mules.
   Ⓑ The animals would gear their speed to suit the walk of the miner.
   Ⓒ both A and B

6. Between what pair of guide words would you find *valve?*
   Ⓐ vamoose/variety
   Ⓑ vague/vapor
   Ⓒ vacate/value

Journeys and Quests

① Word Meanings

Synonyms

1. **intrepid**
   (in trep′ id) *adj.*
   brave and courageous

2. **excursion**
   (ek skûr′ zhən) *n.*
   a short trip

3. **motive**
   (mō′ tiv) *n.*
   reason for doing
   something

4. **mission**
   (mish′ ən) *n.*
   an assigned task
   or service

5. **wayfarer**
   (wā′ fâr′ ər) *n.*
   traveler on foot

6. **mobile**
   (mō′ bəl) *adj.*
   able to move or
   be moved

7. **achievement**
   (ə chēv′ mənt) *n.*
   a goal that has
   been reached

8. **impediment**
   (im ped′ ə mənt) *n.*
   something that slows
   or stops progress

9. **peril**
   (per′ əl) *n.*
   chance or risk of
   danger

10. **messenger**
    (mes′ ən jər) *n.*
    one who brings news

 Circle the synonyms for each vocabulary word below. There may be more than one correct answer.

1. **achievement**
   success
   togetherness
   completion

2. **excursion**
   forgiveness
   trip
   outing

3. **impediment**
   block
   obstruction
   assistance

4. **intrepid**
   courageous
   fearful
   determined

5. **messenger**
   explorer
   courier
   reporter

6. **mission**
   assignment
   government
   effort

7. **mobile**
   portable
   movable
   quick

8. **motive**
   goal
   reason
   achievement

9. **peril**
   darkness
   danger
   risk

10. **wayfarer**
    passerby
    wanderer
    traveler

• •

 ## Think About It

Synonyms are words or phrases that mean the same, or nearly the same thing. What are some other synonyms for the vocabulary words?

② Reference Skills

The Latin Root *ped*

Write the letter of the word that matches each definition below. Use the word parts and their definitions in the box for help.

bi: two	*ment:* state or condition of
centi: hundred	*meter:* something that measures
cure: care	*milli:* thousand
ex: out of	*mo:* motor
im: not	*ped:* foot
ion: act or process	

1. _____ a motor-powered bicycle you can pedal

2. _____ an insect with one thousand legs (an exaggeration)

3. _____ care of the foot, toes, or toenails

4. _____ a trip with a purpose

5. _____ something that blocks progress

6. _____ an instrument that measures distance traveled on foot

7. _____ a walker

8. _____ a hundred-footed insect

9. _____ a lever worked by the foot

10. _____ a two-footed animal

A. pedometer

B. pedal

C. pedicure

D. centipede

E. impediment

F. moped

G. pedestrian

H. biped

I. millipede

J. expedition

Vocabulary List

1. *intrepid*

2. *excursion*

3. *motive*

4. *mission*

5. *wayfarer*

6. *mobile*

7. *achievement*

8. *impediment*

9. *peril*

10. *messenger*

3 Build New Vocabulary

Context Clues

 Read the sentences below and write the vocabulary word that could replace each underlined synonym. Use the context clues in each sentence to help determine the correct word.

1. The broken gear on her bike was an <u>obstruction</u> that kept her from winning the race. _____

2. Receiving extra money was the <u>inducement</u> for finishing the job early. _____

3. The <u>dauntless</u> firefighter saved the two young children.

   _____

4. To be accepted to medical school at the age of 15 is an impressive <u>accomplishment</u>. _____

5. After his leg healed, the <u>ambulatory</u> patient was glad to no longer need the wheelchair. _____

6. The <u>assignment</u> was possible, but it was going to be difficult.

   _____

7. Our family is planning an <u>expedition</u> to London, England, for next year's spring break. _____

8. The officer understood the <u>jeopardy</u> of entering the crime scene. _____

9. The <u>voyager</u> stopped to rest under the shady tree because he was warm and his feet were tired. _____

10. I received the message along with a mysterious package from the <u>courier</u>. _____

Score _____ (Top Score 10)

 **Word Play**

Is It Possible?

 Decide whether each relationship below is possible.
Write *Yes* or *No* in the blank.

1. Could a *mission* be a *peril?* _____

2. Could a *messenger* be *mobile?* _____

3. Would it help to be *intrepid* when facing a *peril?* _____

4. Could an *impediment* be a *messenger?* _____

5. Could a *messenger* be a *wayfarer?* _____

6. Could an *excursion* involve *peril?* _____

7. Could a *peril* have a *motive?* _____

8. Could an *achievement* require a person to be *intrepid?* _____

9. Could you be on a *mission* while on an *excursion?* _____

10. Could a *wayfarer* come across an *impediment?* _____

Match the following vocabulary words with their definitions.

11. _____ mobile   **A.** a short trip made for purpose or pleasure

12. _____ achievement   **B.** a goal that has been successfully reached

13. _____ motive   **C.** a person who delivers messages

14. _____ impediment   **D.** a risk of danger

15. _____ excursion   **E.** a traveler who moves on foot

16. _____ peril   **F.** capable of moving or being moved

17. _____ intrepid   **G.** having or showing no fear; courageous

18. _____ messenger   **H.** something that gets in the way of progress

19. _____ mission   **I.** a goal that causes a person to act

20. _____ wayfarer   **J.** a task or service that is assigned

Vocabulary List

1. **deceased**
   (di sēst') *adj.*
   dead

2. **maternity**
   (mə tûr' ni tē) *n.*
   motherhood

3. **prime**
   (prīm) *adj.*
   of the best quality;
   excellent

4. **graduation**
   (graj' ōō ā' shən) *n.*
   completion of a course
   of study

5. **apprentice**
   (ə pren' tis) *n.*
   learner of a skill

6. **infancy**
   (in' fən sē) *n.*
   babyhood

7. **paternity**
   (pə tûr' ni tē) *n.*
   fatherhood

8. **elderly**
   (el' dər lē) *adj.*
   older

9. **matrimony**
   (mat' rə mō' nē) *n.*
   marriage

10. **juvenile**
    (jōō' və nəl) *adj.*
    young

"Life Stages" Vocabulary

① Word Meanings

Expanded Definitions

 Match each vocabulary word with its expanded definition. Write the letter of the definition in the blank.

1. _____ graduation

2. _____ matrimony

3. _____ juvenile

4. _____ apprentice

5. _____ prime

6. _____ infancy

7. _____ deceased

8. _____ paternity

9. _____ elderly

10. _____ maternity

A. condition or period of being a baby

B. the state of being married

C. past middle age; older

D. the act or state of finishing a degree or schooling

E. first of importance; of the best quality; excellent

F. the state of being a mother; motherhood

G. a person who works for a skilled worker in order to learn a trade

H. the state of being a father; fatherhood

I. childish; youthful

J. dead or expired

 Think About It

The short definitions in your Vocabulary Lists are just the beginning of word knowledge. Exploring words to find their expanded definitions, multiple meanings, and where they originated can be a lot of fun. Linguistics is the scientific study of language. What careers do you think focus on linguistics?

② Reference Skills

Multiple Meanings

Read the dictionary entry for each word below. Then complete each sentence by choosing the word that best fits and write it in the blank. Write the number of the definition you chose in the blank after each sentence.

---

graduation *n.* **1.** the ceremony of giving diplomas to students who have completed a course of study: *The school's graduation will be held in the spring.* **2.** a mark or series of marks showing degrees or other measurements: *The graduation on the thermometer was hard to read.*

juvenile *adj.* **1.** suitable for young children: *Juvenile clothes are next to the boys' department.* **2.** childish; immature: *Quitting a game because you're not winning is juvenile behavior.* **3.** young: *The teacher took her juvenile students to the library.* *n.* **1.** a young person: *A juvenile must appear in court with a parent or guardian.*

prime *adj.* **1.** first in importance; main: *The prime concern of the parents was their child's safety.* **2.** of the best quality; excellent: *I picked these prime strawberries from our garden.* *n.* **1.** the best time or condition: *Tulips are in their prime in early spring.*

---

1. The book that you're looking for is in the

   _____ section of the library. _____

2. The horses at the fair were in _____

   condition. _____

3. The liquid in the beaker reached the highest

   _____ marked on the side. _____

4. The students gave speeches and played musical instruments at

   their _____. _____

Vocabulary List

1. deceased

2. maternity

3. prime

4. graduation

5. apprentice

6. infancy

7. paternity

8. elderly

9. matrimony

10. juvenile

 3 Build New Vocabulary

Word Equations

 Build words related to the vocabulary words by completing the word equations below.

1. pater + *nal* = _____

2. *de* + cease = _____

3. infant + *ile* = _____

4. grade – *e* + *ual* = _____

5. mater + *nal* = _____

6. matron – *on* + *imonial* = _____

• •

 Use the words you made above to complete each sentence below.

7. The cat had a strong _____ instinct and took good care of her kittens.

8. When babies are not given polio shots, they could become sick

with _____ paralysis.

9. Learning a new language is a _____ process.

10. _____ advice is counsel from a father.

11. The couple had an unusual _____ service; they were married on the ski slopes.

12. The _____ of a pet is a sad time that is made easier when it is shared by family and friends.

 **Word Play**

Simple Synonyms

 Write the common word or phrase from the box that is a synonym of each word below. Use a dictionary if you need help.

Common Synonyms			
babyhood	deal	learner	praise
best	fatherhood	marriage	stop working
block	freedom	motherhood	teenager
completion	good	old	youth
dead	job		

1. retire _____

2. apprentice

   _____

3. obstruct

   _____

4. paternity

   _____

5. virtuous

   _____

6. elderly

   _____

7. juvenile

   _____

8. graduation

   _____

9. infancy

   _____

10. employment

    _____

11. maternity

    _____

12. adolescent

    _____

13. matrimony

    _____

14. transaction

    _____

15. deceased

    _____

16. compliment

    _____

17. prime _____

18. emancipation

    _____

"Life Stages" Vocabulary • Word Play   Score _____ (Top Score 18)   Unit 6 • Lesson 32   **129**

1. **frantic**
(fran′ tik) *adj.*
wildly excited by
worry or fear

2. **baffled**
(baf′ əld) *adj.*
puzzled

3. **subdued**
(səb dood′) *adj.*
quieted; lacking
energy

4. **arrogant**
(ar′ ə gənt) *adj.*
overly proud

5. **assured**
(ə shoord′) *adj.*
self-confident

6. **eager**
(ē′ gər) *adj.*
showing great interest
or want

7. **vulnerable**
(vul′ nər ə bəl) *adj.*
capable of being hurt

8. **elated**
(i lā′ tid) *adj.*
joyful

9. **dejected**
(di jek′ tid) *adj.*
sad; depressed

10. **preoccupied**
(prē ok′ yə pīd′) *adj.*
lost in thought

States of Mind

1 Word Meanings

Antonyms

Underline the word in each set below that has the opposite meaning of the boldfaced vocabulary word. Use a dictionary, or thesaurus, if you need help.

1. **frantic**	excited	frenzied	calm
2. **preoccupied**	distracted	focused	inattentive
3. **dejected**	downcast	elated	depressed
4. **baffled**	understands	confused	puzzled
5. **vulnerable**	unprotected	weak	secure
6. **elated**	overjoyed	gloomy	joyous
7. **arrogant**	humble	self-centered	proud
8. **eager**	enthusiastic	ready	unwilling
9. **subdued**	controlled	wild	conquered
10. **assured**	confident	certain	unsure

Match the following vocabulary words with their definitions.

11. _____ assured   **A.** filled with interest, want, and desire

12. _____ preoccupied   **B.** to be brought under control; quieted

13. _____ arrogant   **C.** confident in oneself

14. _____ eager   **D.** feeling or showing too much pride

15. _____ dejected   **E.** bewildered, puzzled, confused

16. _____ baffled   **F.** showing low spirits; depressed

17. _____ vulnerable   **G.** lost in thought

18. _____ subdued   **H.** capable of being easily hurt

② Reference Skills

The Latin Root *ject*

 Write each word from the box below in the blank beside its definition. Use a dictionary if you need help. (**Hint:** Latin definitions are in parentheses.)

reject	inject	interjection
object	deject	adjective

1. to make gloomy (to throw down) _____

2. a word or phrase that expresses feeling (a thing thrown in between) _____

3. to oppose something (to throw in the way)

   _____

4. to say "no" to (to throw back) _____

5. a part of speech that describes a noun (to throw to)

   _____

6. to force something into (to throw in)

   _____

• •

Use the definitions from above and context clues to choose the correct word to complete each sentence below.

7. An exclamation point is used at the end of an

   _____.

8. We _____ to the idea of having homework on the weekends.

9. I have an idea of my own that I want to

   _____ into the discussion.

10. Please do not _____ our suggestion before we can fully explain it.

Vocabulary List

1. frantic
2. baffled
3. subdued
4. arrogant
5. assured
6. eager
7. vulnerable
8. elated
9. dejected
10. preoccupied

 3 Build New Vocabulary

Word Equations

 Complete the word equations below by adding the suffix *-ly* to each adjective to form an adverb. Use a dictionary to check the spelling of your answers.

1. eager + *ly* = _____

2. frantic + *ly* = _____

3. dejected + *ly* = _____

4. arrogant + *ly* = _____

5. assured + *ly* = _____

6. elated + *ly* = _____

· ·

Use the words you formed above to complete each sentence below.

7. The soccer fans _____ awaited the final game of the World Cup.

8. Every player was extremely skillful and handled the ball

    _____ .

9. One player got a yellow card for _____ talking back to the referee when the opposing team was awarded a penalty kick.

10. Although the goalkeeper _____ dove for the ball, he could not save the goal.

11. The teammates shouted with glee and rushed

    _____ to the player who scored the goal.

12. The members of the opposing team just looked

    _____ at one another.

Word Play

Rhyming Riddles

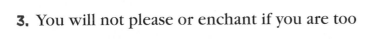

Write the vocabulary word that completes each riddle below.

1. It's expected to feel _____ if you are rejected.

2. Even if your gift is belated, it still could make you feel

   _____.

3. You will not please or enchant if you are too

   _____.

4. If you were stuck alone in the Atlantic, you'd probably feel very

   _____.

5. Your companions might be dissatisfied if you are

   _____.

6. My dog's mood is quite _____ when she has to get shampooed.

7. The kids in the lunch line were hungry and

   _____, so there's not much left, and it's looking meager.

8. Rest _____ that I've matured, and now I'm cured of the silliness you've endured.

9. I bought each and every ticket they raffled but did not win.

   That's why I'm _____.

10. After twisting my ankle, the pain was tolerable, but I was still lying on the ballfield and feeling quite

    _____.

1. overwhelm
(ō′ vər welm′) v.
to defeat completely

2. nuisance
(noo′ səns) n.
a pest

3. tedious
(tē′ dē əs) adj.
boring and repetitive

4. regret
(ri gret′) v.
to feel sorry about

5. contamination
(kən tam′ ə nā′ shən)
n. pollution

6. haughty
(hô′ tē) adj.
overly proud

7. vicious
(vish′ əs) adj.
cruel; wicked

8. agony
(ag′ ə nē) n.
great pain

9. insecurity
(in′ si kyoor′ i tē) n.
lack of self-confidence

10. disaster
(di zas′ tər) n.
sudden misfortune

Vocabulary for Negatives

 **1** **Word Meanings**

Examples

 Each of the items below is an example of one of the vocabulary words. Write each vocabulary word in the blank next to its correct example.

1. polluted water _____

2. a tornado striking a town _____

3. a person who tells lies about others and plots to hurt them

_____

4. feeling bad about forgetting your friend's birthday

_____

5. the feeling of a broken leg _____

6. what the winning team has done to the losing team if the final

score is 50 to 2 _____

7. a proud queen who looks down on her subjects

_____

8. three hours of pulling weeds in your garden

_____

9. being afraid to speak in public _____

10. a swarm of mosquitoes at a picnic

_____

• •

💡 Think About It

Identifying examples of a new word will help you remember the word itself, its meaning, and a context in which to use it.

2 Reference Skills

Prefixes

 Circle the correct definition for each of the following prefixes.

1. *anti-*   two   against   for

2. *bi-*   two   wrong   not

3. *im-*   not   for   half

4. *in-*   half   not   again

5. *mis-*   almost   half   wrong

6. *non-*   not   again   two

7. *pre-*   half   before   for

8. *semi-*   for   almost   again

• •

 Add the correct prefix from above to each word in parentheses below to form a word that fits the sentence context. Use a dictionary to check your answers.

9. If a main character in a story doesn't have any of the positive

   traits of a hero, he is called an (hero) _____.

10. Flying was once thought (possible) _____,
    but now the skies are filled with planes.

11. Even though it takes a longer time, the (direct)

    _____ route is usually more interesting.

12. A (print) _____ is a typing error.

13. A limerick is a funny (sense) _____ poem.

14. A (colon) _____ can be used to correct a
    run-on sentence.

15. A (weekly) _____ newspaper comes every
    two weeks.

Vocabulary List

1. overwhelm

2. nuisance

3. tedious

4. regret

5. contamination

6. haughty

7. vicious

8. agony

9. insecurity

10. disaster

3 Build New Vocabulary

Related Words

Read the passages below. Write the vocabulary word that shares a relationship with the boldfaced related words to complete the sentences.

In an effort to avoid **illness** from drinking poor-quality **water,** you should remember the following **environmental** suggestions: dispose of your pet **waste** properly, use non**toxic** cleansers when washing things **outside,** limit the use of lawn and garden **chemicals,** and protect **natural** growth and landscaping to prevent **soil** erosion. We can control the amount of _____ that affects our water by being educated and practicing **earth**-friendly habits.

_____

In the event of a **natural** _____, whether it is in the form of a raging **tornado,** an exploding **volcano,** a soaring **tsunami,** an **earthquake,** a **drought,** or a **hurricane,** it is important to have a **safety** plan prepared. When **danger** strikes, you may feel **afraid** and **nervous.** These **storms** typically cause many **problems** and can **rarely be avoided.** But it's comforting to know that **organizations** are ready to help with the **recovery** if and when it is needed.

_____

In Hans Christian Andersen's story *The Emperor's New Clothes,* the Emperor was an **overly proud** man with a _____ **attitude.** He was so **concerned** with looking good that he **treated his people poorly.** He **ordered** the finest clothes to be made, but when they were finished, he realized that he could not see them. He was too **conceited** to admit his **fault,** so he "dressed" in the pretend clothes and was made a fool before the entire town.

_____

While sleeping in his tent, Franklin was awakened by an **annoying** mosquito buzzing in his ear. He was sleepy but it was **really bothering** him. He knew he should have closed the tent window but it **didn't work well** and he **didn't want to deal** with it. That mosquito **would not stop** buzzing no matter what Franklin did. It was a **pesky** _____.

_____

4 Word Play

Oxymorons

An **oxymoron** is a phrase made of two words that have opposite meanings or would not usually be used together because their meanings cancel each other out. *Serious fun, cruel kindness,* and *cheerful pessimist* are examples of oxymorons.

 Read the sentences below. Write the word from the box that best completes each oxymoron. The vocabulary words are boldfaced in each sentence.

minor	welcome	pure	excitement

1. Calling the famous 1906 San Francisco, California, earthquake a

   _____ **disaster** would be a misstatement because it caused major destruction to the city.

2. Some people say that children are a _____ **nuisance** because, although they are mischievous, they bring joy to their families' lives.

3. The scientist declared that the amount of oil found in the lake

   was an example of "nothing but _____ **contamination.**"

4. My little brother seems to enjoy the **tedious**

   _____ of playing the same video game for hours and hours.

1. **omit**
   (ō mit´) v.
   to leave out

2. **designate**
   (dez´ ig nāt´) v.
   to name to a position

3. **persecute**
   (pûr´ si kūt´) v.
   to treat cruelly
   and unfairly

4. **execute**
   (ek´ si kūt´) v.
   to carry out, as duties

5. **resign**
   (ri zīn´) v.
   to quit

6. **consecutive**
   (kən sek´ yə tiv) adj.
   following one after
   the other

7. **insignia**
   (in sig´ nē ə) n.
   symbol

8. **dismiss**
   (dis mis´) v.
   to send away

9. **intermission**
   (in´ tər mish´ ən) n.
   a pause between
   events

10. **emit**
    (i mit´) v.
    to give off

Words from Latin

(1) Word Meanings

Latin Origins

 Write each vocabulary word beside its Latin origin word and definition.

Origin Word	Definition	Vocabulary Word
1. signum	a mark, badge	_____
2. exsequi	to follow out	_____
3. resignare	to cancel or unseal	_____
4. consequi	to follow along	_____
5. persqui	to follow through	_____
6. dimissus	to send out	_____
7. intermittere	sent between	_____
8. designare	to indicate or point out for a position	_____
9. omittere	to let go, send	_____
10. emittere	to send out	_____

Complete the following sentences using the Vocabulary List words.

11. The official _____ of the United States is an eagle with outstretched wings.

12. A president of the United States can serve only two

    _____ terms.

② Reference Skills

Phonetic Spelling

Underline the correct phonetic spelling of each vocabulary word below.

1. **consecutive**	kən sek´ yə tiv	con sek´ yə tive	kən sec´ yew tiv
2. **designate**	dez´ egg nate´	des´ igg nāt´	dez´ ig nāt´
3. **dismiss**	des miss´	dəs məss´	dis mis´
4. **emit**	e´ mit	i mit´	e met´
5. **execute**	ek´ si kūt´	ek se kute´	ex´ si cut
6. **insignia**	in signə a	en sig´ ni a	in sig´ nē ə
7. **intermission**	in´ tər mish´ ən	en´ tər mish ən	in´ ter mesh´ ion
8. **persecute**	per´ se kūt´	pûr´ si kūt´	pûr´ si cute´
9. **omit**	ö mət´	ō mōt´	ō mit´
10. **resign**	rē´ sign	ri zīn´	re´ zine

Match the following vocabulary words with their definitions.

11. _____ designate   **A.** to send away or allow to leave

12. _____ resign   **B.** to give cruel, harmful, or unjust treatment

13. _____ dismiss   **C.** a badge, medal, or other symbol of position

14. _____ consecutive   **D.** to point out by a mark, sign, or name

15. _____ intermission   **E.** following one after another without a break

16. _____ insignia   **F.** to carry out; fulfill

17. _____ emit   **G.** to send forth or give off; discharge

18. _____ omit   **H.** to give up a job, position, or office by choice

19. _____ persecute   **I.** the short period of time between events

20. _____ execute   **J.** to leave out; fail to include

Vocabulary List

1. *omit*

2. *designate*

3. *persecute*

4. *execute*

5. *resign*

6. *consecutive*

7. *insignia*

8. *dismiss*

9. *intermission*

10. *emit*

3 Build New Vocabulary

The Latin Root *sign*

 Match each word below to its correct definition. Write the letter of the definition in the blank.

1. assignment _____

2. design _____

3. reassign _____

4. signature _____

5. signify _____

A. to give a new task to

B. to be a symbol; to mean

C. a plan

D. a person's name written by him or her

E. a given task

 Complete each sentence below by writing the correct word from above.

6. In 1791 Major Pierre Charles L'Enfant made the

_____ for the streets of Washington, D.C.

7. The _____ of John Hancock stands out from all the others on the Declaration of Independence.

8. The stars on the American flag _____ the 50 states of the Union.

9. A person who works for the State Department may have an

_____ in a foreign country.

10. It is common for the head of the State Department to

_____ diplomats from one job to another.

Score _____ (Top Score 10) Words from Latin • Build New Vocabulary

 ④ **Word Play**

Crossword Puzzle

 Use the clues below to complete the crossword puzzle.

Across

2. to quit
6. following one after another
8. to leave out
10. a pause between events

Down

1. to treat in a cruel way
3. to carry out
4. to send away
5. to name
7. a symbol
9. to give off

Vocabulary Review

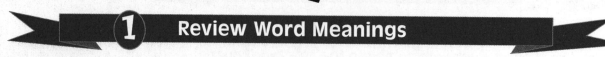

① Review Word Meanings

Read the passage below. Then answer the questions about the boldfaced vocabulary words.

Christopher Columbus's Mission

In 1492, the King and Queen of Spain **designated** Christopher Columbus as their representative and sent him on a **mission** to China. Columbus was **elated** because he had been trying to convince them for a long time to finance his trip.

The King and Queen's **motive** for sending Columbus to the Far East was to get valuable spices and other riches. Columbus was **intrepid** and had no **insecurity** about the success of his trip. He felt **assured** that he would overcome any **impediment** and that his journey would be a great **achievement** for Spain.

Now read the following questions. Then completely fill in the bubble of the correct answer.

1. Which of the following sets of words includes prefixes that mean "not"?
   Ⓐ designated, motive, pursuit
   Ⓑ insecurity, intrepid, impediment
   Ⓒ achievement, mission, elated

2. What is the relationship between *insecurity* and *assured*?
   Ⓐ They have the same meanings.
   Ⓑ They have opposite meanings.
   Ⓒ They have unrelated meanings.

3. Which of the following words means "the reason for doing something"?
   Ⓐ mission
   Ⓑ pursuit
   Ⓒ motive

4. Which of the following is a synonym of *elated?*
   Ⓐ overjoyed
   Ⓑ dejected
   Ⓒ overly proud

5. In which of the following sentences is *designated* used correctly?
   Ⓐ Queen Isabella and King Ferdinand designated Columbus with money and supplies.
   Ⓑ Queen Isabella and King Ferdinand designated if Columbus could reach China.
   Ⓒ Queen Isabella and King Ferdinand designated Columbus to sail to China.

6. Which of the following is not an example of an *impediment?*
   Ⓐ a peril
   Ⓑ a graduation
   Ⓒ a nuisance

7. What is the definition for *pursuit?*
   Ⓐ chase after
   Ⓑ an interest one enjoys
   Ⓒ a and b

8. What is the antonym for *achievement?*
   Ⓐ fail to complete
   Ⓑ goal reached
   Ⓒ task completed successfully

 **② Review Word Meanings**

Read the passage below. Then answer the questions about the boldfaced vocabulary words.

Columbus's Voyages

Columbus set sail for the Far East with three ships. One of the duties that he was to **execute** for the King and Queen was to serve as their **messenger** to the ruler of China. Before Columbus was **dismissed,** he was given a letter stamped with the **insignia** of Queen Isabella and King Ferdinand and addressed to the Chinese ruler.

As the long and **tedious** journey went on, Columbus's crew became **dejected** because their supplies were running low and no land was in sight. When the ships landed on a Caribbean island instead of China, Columbus was **baffled** and made many **excursions** to other islands in search of China.

Columbus returned to Spain and had no **regrets** about his journey because he was certain he had reached islands near Asia. He was **eager** to continue his search for a route to China, and he made three more **consecutive** voyages.

Now read the following questions. Then completely fill in the bubble of the correct answer.

1. Which of the following words has a Latin root that means "mark" or "symbol"?
   - Ⓐ messenger
   - Ⓑ insignia
   - Ⓒ dejected

2. Which of the following is a definition of *execute?*
   - Ⓐ to explore
   - Ⓑ to give up a position
   - Ⓒ to carry out

3. Which of the following means the opposite of *dejected?*
   - Ⓐ elated
   - Ⓑ tedious
   - Ⓒ baffled

4. If several excursions are *consecutive,* they _____.
   - Ⓐ are unsuccessful
   - Ⓑ are long and difficult
   - Ⓒ occur one after the other

5. Which of the following meanings of the word *dismiss* is used in the passage above?
   - Ⓐ to give an action of law without further hearing
   - Ⓑ to fire from a job
   - Ⓒ sent away

6. Which of the following is a synonym for *eager?*
   - Ⓐ frantic
   - Ⓑ ready and willing
   - Ⓒ arrogant

7. In which sentence below is *regrets* used in the correct context?
   - Ⓐ They had no regrets about their journey.
   - Ⓑ She regrets the fact that there wasn't time to study more.
   - Ⓒ a and b

8. Which of the following is the correct phonetic spelling for *insignia?*
   - Ⓐ in sig´ nē ə
   - Ⓑ en sig´ nī ə
   - Ⓒ en seg´ ne ə

Vocabulary Review   Score _____ (Top Score 8)   Unit 6 • Lesson 36   **143**

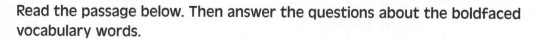

③ Review Word Meanings

Read the passage below. Then answer the questions about the boldfaced vocabulary words.

The Spanish Conquerors

Soon after Christopher Columbus's voyages, many Spanish soldiers made the long and perilous journey to what they now knew was the New World. The soldiers were very **haughty** and soon became **preoccupied** with **persecuting** the native peoples of the islands. Some Spanish soldiers pretended to be friendly to the natives but soon became **vicious** toward them and even made them slaves.

The people Columbus had described as friendly and generous toward the Spanish now realized that the Spanish discovery of their islands was a **disaster.** The natives were now dejected because they had been **subdued** by the **arrogant** Spanish soldiers.

Now read the following questions. Then completely fill in the bubble of the correct answer.

1. Which of the following is a definition of *persecute?*
   Ⓐ to overcome by force
   Ⓑ to become friends with
   Ⓒ to treat cruelly and unfairly

2. Which set of words below contains only synonyms of *haughty?*
   Ⓐ proud, arrogant, snobbish
   Ⓑ proud, cruel, vicious
   Ⓒ dishonest, dishonorable, disgraceful

3. The natives were _____ by the _____ Spanish soldiers.
   Ⓐ calmed, peaceful
   Ⓑ thrilled, entertaining
   Ⓒ overpowered, conceited

4. Which of the following is a definition of *preoccupied?*
   Ⓐ long and boring
   Ⓑ lost in thought
   Ⓒ exciting

5. Which of the following is a synonym of *vicious?*
   Ⓐ dishonest
   Ⓑ proud
   Ⓒ cruel

6. Which of the following words are related to *corrupt?*
   Ⓐ dishonest, shady, crooked
   Ⓑ large, huge, positive
   Ⓒ honest, pleasant, enjoyable

7. In which sentence below is *disaster* used correctly?
   Ⓐ The discovery of the islands was a disaster for the natives.
   Ⓑ The discovery of the islands was disaster natives.
   Ⓒ a and b

8. What context clue helps you understand the meaning of the word *vicious* in the passage above?
   Ⓐ Some Spanish soldiers
   Ⓑ pretended to be friendly
   Ⓒ became vicious

4 Review Word Meanings

Read the passage below. Then answer the questions about the boldfaced vocabulary words.

Destruction of the Caribbean Natives

The natives of the Caribbean islands were in even greater **peril** than they had realized. The Spanish soldiers unknowingly brought **contamination** to the islands in the form of diseases. The natives were **vulnerable** and many became sick and died.

At first only the weak and **elderly** natives and those in their **infancy** died of these diseases. But later, even young men in the **prime** of their lives were overcome by **agony** and then death. By the end of the 1500s, about 90 percent of the native population was **deceased.** As the Spanish became more **mobile,** the natives paid a terrible price for their discovery of the New World.

Now read the following questions. Then completely fill in the bubble of the correct answer.

1. Which of the following provides two correct definitions of *prime?*
   Ⓐ of the best quality; at the best time
   Ⓑ youth; paternity
   Ⓒ at the best time; during a learning period

2. Which of the following means "great pain"?
   Ⓐ peril
   Ⓑ vulnerable
   Ⓒ agony

3. What is the relationship between *infancy* and *elderly?*
   Ⓐ They are the beginning and ending stages in a person's life.
   Ⓑ They are the last two stages in a person's life.
   Ⓒ They are consecutive stages in a person's life.

4. Which of the following is a definition of *vulnerable?*
   Ⓐ polluted
   Ⓑ in great danger
   Ⓒ able to be harmed

5. Which of the following means the opposite of *peril?*
   Ⓐ danger
   Ⓑ safety
   Ⓒ slavery

6. What word is a synonym for *contamination?*
   Ⓐ impediment
   Ⓑ pollution
   Ⓒ excursion

7. Which sentence below has the correct usage for *deceased?*
   Ⓐ About 90 percent of the native population was deceased.
   Ⓑ The deceased was a native of the island.
   Ⓒ a and b

8. Which of the following meanings for the word *vulnerable* is used in the passage above?
   Ⓐ capable of being emotionally hurt; sensitive
   Ⓑ capable of being physically hurt or wounded
   Ⓒ open to attack; not protected externally

Cumulative Review

Definitions

 Write the vocabulary word that matches each definition below. (**Hint:** The vocabulary words may appear in any lesson throughout the book.)

1. a period of ten years *n.* _____

2. a secret, illegal plan *n.* _____

3. freedom from control *n.* _____

4. a tooth on a gear *n.* _____

5. a tropical hurricane *n.* _____

6. pollution *n.* _____

7. the overthrow of a government *n.* _____

8. very pleasing or delicious *adj.* _____

9. far beyond normal human ability *adj.*

_____

10. relating to the sky *adj.* _____

11. a pause between events *n.* _____

12. to speak in a low, soft voice *v.* _____

13. one who is second in charge *n.* _____

14. going beyond limits; shocking *adj.* _____

15. a list of goods in stock *n.* _____

Score _____ (Top Score 15)

② Word Meanings

Synonyms

Choose the vocabulary word from the box that is a synonym for each word below. Write the vocabulary word in the blank. (**Hint:** Each word is used once.)

luminous	domain	enlist	counsel	mission
compliment	thwart	elated	frigid	redeem
frail	transaction	bewilder	foe	tepid

1. overjoyed _____

2. join _____

3. warm _____

4. reclaim _____

5. cold _____

6. bright _____

7. quest _____

8. confuse _____

9. praise _____

10. property _____

11. enemy _____

12. prevent _____

13. fragile _____

14. advice _____

15. deal _____

Score _____ (Top Score 15)   Cumulative Review   **147**

Sentence Completion

Write the vocabulary word that best completes each sentence below. Each sentence contains a clue related to a lesson theme. (**Hint:** The vocabulary words may appear in any lesson throughout the book.)

1. Susan B. Anthony encouraged many women to get involved in politics when she fought for women's _____.

2. Because our science project was not finished, we asked our teacher to _____ our free time.

3. When writing in our journals about our good traits, I wrote that I have _____ because I help out at the shelter every Saturday with my aunt.

4. He was a _____ who traveled south after the Civil War to take advantage of the financial and political disorder.

5. Visual art affects people in different ways depending on their _____, or how they see it.

6. The tour guide told us that the *Snow Squall* is the only survivor of the American-built _____ ships. It was used for sailing quickly during the Gold Rush Era.

7. During _____, a baby will grow faster and learn more than during any other life stage afterward.

8. It is important that your body gets enough _____ and energy from healthy foods before exercising.

9. I love to see the _____ win a competition because it surprises everyone.

10. She had an _____ feeling that the mystery would never be solved.

Words and Themes

 Choose two words from the box that belong in each theme below. Write the words in the blank. Try to complete the exercise without looking at the Vocabulary List in each lesson.

1. **Vocabulary for Organization** _____

2. **"Heritage" Vocabulary** _____

3. **Vocabulary for the Senses** _____

4. **Machines and Tools** _____

5. **Journeys & Quests** _____

6. **Vocabulary for Problems** _____

7. **The Human Voice** _____

8. **Making a New Nation** _____

9. **"Good Traits" Vocabulary** _____

10. **"Competition" Vocabulary** _____

11. **"Astronomy" Vocabulary** _____

12. **"Life Stages" Vocabulary** _____

13. **"Going West" Vocabulary** _____

14. **"Cooperation" Vocabulary** _____

15. **Economy Vocabulary** _____

excursion
citizenship
gracious
boomtown
pursue
enterprise
generator
Confederate
constellation
juvenile
bellow
banter
compartment
meteor
compromise
dilemma
forty-niner
budget
inheritance
confidence
tolerate
diesel
structure
battlefield
elderly
shrill
alternative
dominate
insult
messenger

Word Maps

You can draw a **word map** to help you understand what a word means and remember how to use it in a sentence, or context. The word map below is for a vocabulary word in this book.

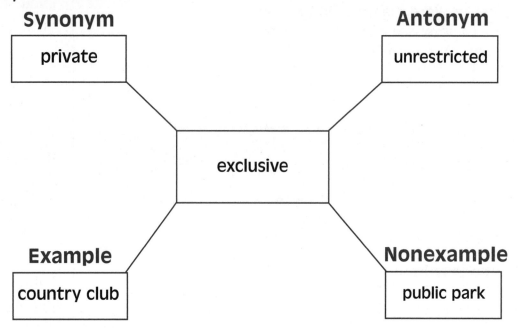

Synonym
private

Antonym
unrestricted

exclusive

Example
country club

Nonexample
public park

Vocabulary Word Used in an Example Sentence: *Most country clubs are exclusive, which means that not everyone can be a member.*

A **Venn diagram** can help you compare and contrast two words. When you draw a Venn diagram, write the features that the words share where the circles overlap. In the outer part of each circle, write the features that only that word has.

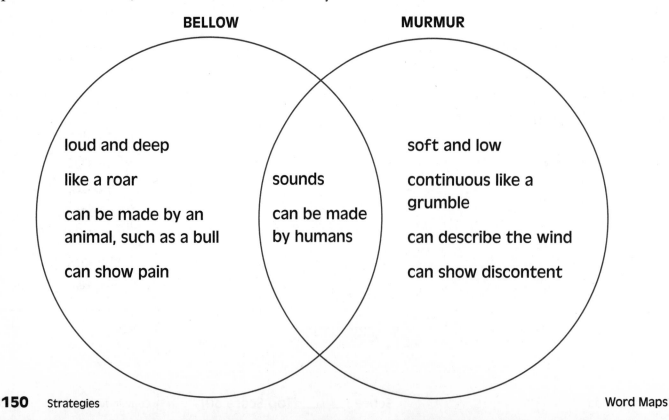

BELLOW

MURMUR

loud and deep

like a roar

can be made by an animal, such as a bull

can show pain

sounds

can be made by humans

soft and low

continuous like a grumble

can describe the wind

can show discontent

Categorization

A **category** is a kind of group. By placing words into categories, you can see how they are related, which will help you remember their meanings. The list below includes words that do not seem to be related.

politician	epidemic	ballot
prolong	decade	immune
vaccinate	polls	continual
suffrage	interval	propaganda
eternal	sterile	diagnosis

Here is the same set of words organized into categories.

Words Related to Politics

politician

polls

ballot

suffrage

propaganda

Time Words

eternal

prolong

decade

interval

continual

Words Related to Health

epidemic

vaccinate

sterile

immune

diagnosis

Context Clues

You will learn many new words from reading. **Context clues** are words, phrases, and sentences that tell something about an unknown word. Sometimes context clues clearly tell a word's meaning, but other times they only hint at it.

Steps for Using Context Clues

1. Find the unknown word.
2. List the words or phrases that tell something about its meaning.
3. Reread the sentence that contains the unknown word and list clues found in that sentence. If you need more clues, reread the sentences before and after the one that contains the unknown word and list those clues.
4. Guess the meaning of the unknown word based on your list of clues.

The following is a list of some types of context clues.

Definition Context Clues

The definition, or meaning, of the unknown word might be in the sentence or nearby sentences.

The *intrepid*, or fearless, captain led his soldiers into battle.

Intrepid is defined in the sentence as "fearless."

Clue Words: *or, in other words, that is, which is, which means*

Example Context Clues

There might be examples of the unknown word in the sentence or nearby sentences.

Subterranean* animals, such as earthworms and cicada nymphs, are an important part of the life cycle.

Earthworms and *cicada nymphs* are examples of *subterranean* animals because they live underground.

Subterranean means "being, located, or happening below the surface of the earth."

Clue Words: *for example, for instance, including, like, such as*

Cause-and-Effect Context Clues

An unknown word might be explained as part of a cause-and-effect relationship.

I walked into the wrong classroom because I was *baffled* by the new schedule.

Being baffled is the cause, and the effect is *walking into the wrong classroom.* You can tell from the sentence that *baffled* means "confused or perplexed."

Clue Words: *as a result, because, consequently, therefore, thus*

Context Clues

Comparison Context Clues

The unknown word might be compared to a word or phrase that has the same meaning. To compare is to find similarities among things.

> **Kelton thought the machine would *emit* fumes into the room. I also thought it would give off unwanted gases.**

Emit means "to give off." In the sentences above, Kelton and the other speaker thought the same thing would happen.

Clue Words: *also, same, resembling, identical, similarly, too, likewise, like*

Contrast Context Clues

The unknown word might be contrasted with another word or phrase. To contrast is to find differences among things.

> **Instead of being *comrades,* the two politicians became enemies.**

Comrades are contrasted with *enemies* in the sentence. A comrade is a close friend or companion.

Clue Words: *however, but, instead of, on the other hand, unlike*

General Context Clues

Sometimes there are not specific clues in a sentence that will help you figure out the meaning of an unknown word. In this case, you can use the details in the words or sentences surrounding the unknown word; this is called using the general context.

> **Our family is excited about our new *imported* furniture. We will pick it up from the boat that has just arrived from New Zealand.**

The first sentence tells you that the furniture is *imported.* The second sentence mentions that the furniture will be on a boat coming from New Zealand. An import is something that comes from another country.

Word Relationships

Synonyms

A **synonym** is a word or phrase that means the same, or nearly the same, as another word. The words *plead* and *beg* are synonyms.

> **We will *plead* for extra recess time.**
> **We will *beg* for extra recess time.**

The sentences above mean the same thing. Remember that many synonyms do not have *exactly* the same meaning and that substituting one word for another without checking its specific definition might change what is being said.

> **The *redolent* roses in my grandmother's garden make it a pleasant place to be.**
> **The *smelly* roses in my grandmother's garden make it a pleasant place to be.**

The words *redolent* and *smelly* are listed as synonyms in most thesauruses. However, *redolent* usually means "sweet smelling," and *smelly* suggests a bad smell.

Antonyms

An **antonym** is a word or phrase that has the opposite meaning of another word. For example, the words *virtuous* and *wicked* are antonyms.

> **The knights were known for their *virtuous* deeds.**
> **The knights were known for their *wicked* deeds.**

Changing the word *virtuous* to its antonym *wicked* changes the meaning of the sentence.

Word Relationships

Homographs

Homographs are words that are spelled the same but have different meanings and sometimes have different pronunciations.

> **She had to quickly *duck* when she saw the *duck* flying straight at her.**

> **It will be *close*, but I think I will get to the store before they *close*.**

> **What do you call a fish that has a very deep singing voice? (a *bass bass*)**

Homophones

Homophones are words that sound the same but have different meanings and are usually spelled differently. Be sure to look up these words in a dictionary to check your spelling. Remember that a computer's spell check will not find these to be incorrect.

> **The color of that *wood would* look great in my bedroom.**

> **As we *towed* the rowboat out of the water, we noticed a *toad* sitting inside.**

> **What is part of the whole? (*some* of the *sum*)**

Related Words

Related words are words that have the same base word or root word. They are related in meaning. Look at the examples below.

> **destination:** a place to which a person is going
> **destiny:** what happens to a person or thing; fortune

> **prime:** of the best quality
> **primary:** first in order, as in *primary school*
> **primitive:** of, relating to, or characteristic of an early original stage, especially in the development of something

Word Relationships
Analogies

An **analogy** shows how two pairs of words are related. To complete an analogy, look at the first pair of words and decide how they relate to each other. The second pair of words relates in the same way, so you need to choose a word that shows the same relationship.

The following is an analogy: *cog : gear :: finger : hand.* It is read like this: *cog* is to *gear* as *finger* is to *hand.*

There are many different types of analogies. Listed below are some common forms with examples for each.

Antonym Analogies

The words in each pair are antonyms.

omit : add :: up : down

publicly : privately :: opened : closed

Part-Whole Analogies

The first word in each pair is part of the second word.

department : company :: yolk : egg

ship : armada :: student : class

Synonym Analogies

The words in each pair are synonyms.

resign : quit :: divide : separate

sterile : pure :: danger : peril

Object-Use Analogies

The first word in each pair is an object, and the second word tells what you do with it.

ballot : vote :: book : read

piano : play :: food : eat

Cause-and-Effect Analogies

The first word in each pair is the cause, and the second word is the effect.

precipitation : wet :: study : learn

provoke : anger :: tired : sleep

BUILDING
Vocabulary
Skills

Level 5
Notebook Reference

To Reinforce Vocabulary Skills

Tools and Reference

Table of Contents

Word Origins

Origin means "beginning" or "source." The origin of a word is where and when the word was first used. Many English words come from words that were first used in ancient Rome, where people spoke Latin. English words also come from other languages, such as Greek, French, German, and Spanish.

A dictionary entry might include the origin of the entry word. It may also list the date when the word was first used in the English language. An entry that includes the origin of a word will look like this:

> **cease** /sēs′/ *v.* [*French,* from *cesser, Latin,* from *cessare,* to hold back] (14c): to come to an end; stop.

The dictionary entry above tells you that *cease* was first used in the English language in the 1300s (the fourteenth century). It also tells you that *cease* came from two languages—first Latin, then French.

The next dictionary entry includes the origin of the word *armada.*

> **ar ma da** /är mä′ də/ *n.* [*Spanish, Medieval Latin,* from *armata,* army, fleet] (1533): a large fleet of warships.

Armada came from Medieval Latin (a form of the Latin language spoken during a specific period of time) and from Spanish. It was first used in English in 1533.

Prefixes and Suffixes

Prefixes

Prefixes are added to the beginning of base words or root words to make new words.

Prefix	Meaning	Examples
bi-	two	bicycle, biannual, bifocal
cent-	one hundred	century, centipede, centimeter
co-	together	coordinate, cooperate, co-chair
dis-	not; opposite	discharge, dismiss, disagree
in-, im-	not	inactive, indivisible, immature
in-, im-	in; into	include, import, implant
multi-	many	multicolored, multimedia, multicultural
pre-	before	preoccupied, precaution, prefix
pro-	forward; favor	provoke, proceed, provide
re-	again	rethink, rewrite, reappear
super-	above; beyond	supersede, supervisor, superhuman
trans-	across	transcontinental, transfer, translate
un-	not	unable, unchanged, unofficial

Suffixes

Suffixes are added to the end of base words or root words to make new words.

Suffix	Meaning	Examples
-able, -ible	is; can be	notable, calculable, accessible
-er, -or	one who	wayfarer, director, astronomer
-ful	full of	joyful, careful, thoughtful
-ify	make; form into	terrify, beautify, falsify
-ive	inclined to	active, exclusive, positive
-less	without	fearless, hopeless, ageless
-ment	state or quality of	employment, astonishment, achievement
-ness	state or quality of	eagerness, awareness, goodness
-ous	full of	virtuous, outrageous, joyous

Root Words

A **root word** is the basic part of a word that gives the word its meaning. You can add a prefix, suffix, or both to a root word. If you do not know what a word means, look for its root.

Root Word	Word Forms
comfort	uncomfortable, discomfort, comforting, comfortable
view	preview, viewer, viewed, review
tolerate	tolerance, intolerance, tolerated

Greek and Latin Roots

Some root words come from the Greek and Latin languages. Many Greek and Latin roots cannot stand alone as words in English. Like all root words, though, Greek and Latin roots having a meaning.

Greek Roots

Root	Meaning	Words
bio	life	biology, biography
cycl	circle; ring	bicycle, recycle
gen	birth; race	genetic, generation
onym	name	synonym, antonym
photo	light	photograph, photosynthesis
phon	sound	telephone, symphony

Latin Roots

Root	Meaning	Words
aqua	water	aquarium, aquamarine
ject	throw	project, eject
min	small; less	minimum, minor
ped	foot	expedition, pedestrian
sect	cut	intersect, dissect
sign	mark	signature, insignia
struct	build	structure, construction
vac	empty	vacant, evacuate
voc	voice	vocal, advocate

Australian, Indian, and Sanskrit Words

Many words have been borrowed from other languages or cultures and are used in the English language. Occasionally the spelling is changed from its original form. The list below includes words that come from Australia and India (Sanskrit is an ancient Indian language).

Australian Words

boomerang	a flat curved piece of wood that can return to the thrower
dingo	a wild dog that looks like a wolf
kangaroo	Australian marsupial mammal that has powerful hind legs
koala	a chubby, tailless Australian animal that lives mainly in trees
wombat	a burrowing mammal that is active at night

Indian Words

bandana	dyed cloth
bungalow	a one-storied house with a low-pitched roof
cheetah	an animal in the cat family
indigo	a deep blue color
jodhpur	riding pants named after the town in which they were first made
khaki	a dull, tan color
loot	valuable goods taken in war
pajamas	nightclothes
sari	a long piece of fabric wrapped and worn as an outer garment

Sanskrit Words

karma	the effect of all your actions
nirvana	highest state of happiness
yoga	exercise of the body and mind

Australian, Indian, and Sanskrit Words

Figurative Language

Figurative language is the use of words in a creative way to mean something different from the usual meanings of words. Common types of figurative language are shown below.

Hyperbole, or Exaggeration

A **hyperbole** is an exaggeration used to make a point.

Example: *I melted at the baseball game yesterday.*

Did the person really melt at the game? No. This hyperbole just tells you that he or she was very hot.

Idioms

An **idiom** is an expression, or a colorful way of saying something. It cannot be understood by the meanings of the actual words.

Example: *Yoko's new car turned out to be a lemon.*

Yoko was not really driving a lemon around town. Saying that something is a lemon means that it does not work well. Other idiomatic expressions include "It's time to hit the hay" (it's time to sleep) and "Let's get the ball rolling" (let's get started).

Similes

A **simile** compares two things that are not the same by using the words *like* or *as*.

Example: *Zach and his sister fight like cats and dogs.*

This sentence compares Zack and his sister to cats and dogs to explain how they fight.

Metaphors

A **metaphor** compares two things that are not the same without using the words *like* or *as*.

Example: *My teacher is a walking encyclopedia.*

This sentence compares a teacher to an encyclopedia, which means that he or she is very knowledgeable.

Reference Skills

The Parts of a Dictionary Entry

Study the parts of the dictionary entry below. Some dictionary entries may not include *all* the information shown in the sample entry.

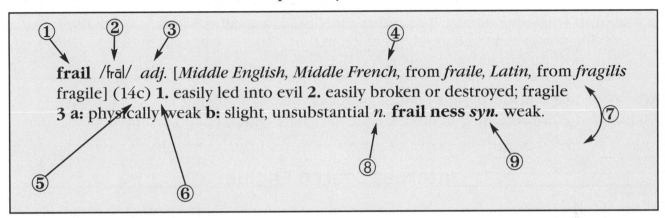

1. **Entry Word with Syllabication** – shows how to spell the word and how many syllables the word has
2. **Phonetic Spelling** – shows how to say the word
3. **Part of Speech** – shows the part of speech, which tells you how to use the word in a sentence
4. **Word Origin** – tells where the word was first used
5. **Date of First Use in English** – tells when the word was first used in the English language (*c* means "century")
6. **Most Common Definition** – gives the definition that is used most often in English
7. **Other Definitions** – gives other definitions, or multiple meanings, for the word
8. **Other Forms** –shows other forms of the word
9. **Synonym** – gives one or more synonyms for the word

Most dictionaries use abbreviations in their entries. There should be a list of these abbreviations with each full meaning near the front or back of the dictionary.

Reference Skills

Thesaurus

You can use a **thesaurus** to find synonyms, or words or phrases that have the same or nearly the same meaning. You will most likely find antonyms, or words with opposite meanings, listed as well. Below you will find a sample thesaurus entry:

> **omit** *v. Please omit my name from your list:* leave out, exclude, except, miss, skip, pass over, forget about, preclude, ignore, delete, drop, cut, set aside. ***Ant.*** include, put in, add, remember, recall.

When you use a thesaurus, it is important to look up a synonym or antonym in a dictionary before you use it to make sure it fits in the context of your sentence.

Internet Search Engine

Using the **Internet** as a research tool offers a large amount of information at a very fast pace. Be sure to spell your keyword search correctly and be as specific as possible. Sometimes a successful search will require more than one attempt, but most will offer at least one link to a related site.

Encyclopedia

An **encyclopedia** includes articles on many different topics. These articles are listed in alphabetical order. An encyclopedia provides you with more information than a dictionary entry. Most encyclopedias are printed in many volumes, and most have an index to help you locate your information quickly.

Rhyming Dictionary

A **rhyming dictionary** lists words that rhyme. If you were writing a song or a poem and needed a word that rhymes with *eerie,* you could look in a rhyming dictionary and find words such as *cheery, dreary, leery, smeary, teary,* or *weary.*

| 1 | 2 | 3 | 4 | 5 | 6 | 7 | 8 | 9 | 10 | 11 | 12 | 13 | 14 | 15 | 16 | 17 | 18 | 19 | 20 |
| A | B | C | D | E-F | G | H-I | J | K | L | M | N | O | P-Q | R | S | T | U-V | W | X-Z |

Parts of Speech

Nouns

Nouns name everything. For example, nouns name persons, places, things (this includes animals), and ideas. Examples of nouns are divided into categories below.

Person	Place	Thing	Idea
boy	America	pencil	freedom
Abby	museum	building	love
chief	space	frog	peace

Pronouns

Pronouns can replace a noun or nouns. The sentence, *Seth forgot Seth's notebook back in Seth's classroom* could use the pronoun *his* to say, *Seth forgot* his *notebook back in* his *classroom.*

Verbs

Verbs show action, state of being, or ownership. *Dominate* is an action verb that means "to control." *Is, was, were, be, being,* and *been* are some examples of state of being verbs. *Have* shows ownership.

Adjectives

Adjectives describe nouns or pronouns. Adjectives usually answer one of the following questions: *What kind? Which one? How much? How many?*

The ambitious person finished first.

Ambitious is the adjective describing the noun *person.*

Adverbs

Adverbs describe verbs, adjectives, or other adverbs. Adverbs usually answer one of the following questions: *When? Where? How? Why? Under what conditions? To what extreme?*

He answered quickly.

Quickly is the adverb describing the verb *answered.* It tells how he answered.

Prepositions

Prepositions show the relationship of nouns or pronouns to other words in a sentence.

We drove through the tunnel. The bag is under the table.

Conjunctions

Conjunctions connect words or simple sentences to each other. Some conjunctions are *and, or, nor, but,* and *yet.*

Glossary

A

ab nor mal /ab nor′ məl/ *adj.* different from the usual. *My cat acts like a dog and often displays abnormal behavior.*

ac com mo date /ə kom′ ə dāt′/ *v.* **accommodates, accommodating, accommodated. 1.** to help. *The park guide accommodated us when we asked for the name of a good motel.* **2.** to hold or have room for. *Our auditorium accommodates 250 people.*

a chieve ment /ə chēv′ mənt/ *n.* a goal that has been reached; something accomplished. *The development of a vaccine for smallpox was a great achievement.*

ac knowl edge /ak nol′ ij/ *v.* **acknowledges, acknowledging, acknowledged. 1.** to admit. *My sister acknowledged that she had borrowed my blue sweater.* **2.** to express thanks for. *The actor acknowledged the applause by bowing to the audience.*

act /akt/ *n.* **1.** something done; a deed. *Rescuing a drowning man is an act of bravery.* **2.** the process of doing something. *I caught my brother in the act of taking cookies from the cookie jar.* **3.** one of the main parts of a play, opera, or ballet. *The last act of the opera amused the audience.*

ad vo cate /ad′ və kit/ *n.* a person who openly supports a person or a cause. *Mahatma Gandhi was an advocate of nonviolence.*

a gen da /ə jən′ də/ *n.* a list of things to do. *The students prepared an agenda for the next drama club meeting.*

ag gres sion /ə gresh′ ən/ *n.* a hostile attack. *Acts of aggression often lead to wars between countries.*

ag on y /ag′ ə nē/ *n., pl.* **agonies.** great pain or suffering of the body or mind. *He was in agony when he broke his leg.*

al le giance /ə lē ′ jəns/ *n.* loyalty to a country or ruler. *To pledge allegiance to a country means to promise to be loyal to that country.*

al li ance /ə lī′ əns/ *n.* an agreement to join together. *Two small countries will sometimes form an alliance to protect each other's interests.*

al ter na tive /ôl tûr′ nə tiv/ *n., pl.* **alternatives.** a choice between things. *We were offered the alternative of traveling by train.*

am bi tious /am bish′ əs/ *adj.* strongly driven or eager to succeed at something. *The ambitious governor said he would run for president.*

a nat om y /ə nat′ ə mē/ *n., pl.* **anatomies. 1.** the structure of organisms. *We are studying the anatomy of mammals in science class.* **2.** the science that deals with the structure of animals or plants. *My uncle studies anatomy in medical school.*

an ces try /an′ ses trē/ *n.* the past generations of one's family. *I am of Scotch-Irish ancestry.*

an nounce /ə nouns′/ *v.* **announces, announcing, announced.** to make known publicly. *The principal announced that school would close early that day.*

ap pli ance /ə plī′ əns/ *n.* a household machine with a particular use. *Toasters and irons are small appliances.*

ap pren tice /ə pren′ tis/ *n.* a person who works for a skilled worker in order to learn a trade or an art. *Before working independently, an electrician works as an apprentice.*

ap prox i mate /ə prok′ sə mit/ *adj.* nearly correct. *My dog's approximate weight is 12 pounds.* /ə prok′ sə māt′/ *v.* **approximates, approximating, approximated.** to estimate. *Can you approximate the time it will take you to finish painting the room?*

ar bi trar y /är′ bi trer′ ē/ *adj.* **1.** based on chance rather than reason. *We made an arbitrary decision to walk home a different way.* **2.** based on opinion rather than on a rule or a reason. *Decisions in courts of law should not be arbitrary.*

ar id /ar′ id/ *adj.* dry; getting very little rain. *One fifth of Earth's land is arid desert.*

ar ma da /är mä′ də/ *n.* a large fleet of warships. *Philip II of Spain sent the Spanish Armada to England in 1588.*

ar ro gant /ar′ ə gənt/ *adj.* showing or having too much pride or feelings of superiority. *His arrogant way of talking kept him from having many friends.*

as sump tion /ə sump′ shən/ *n.* something taken as truth. *My assumption that the girl did not like me was wrong.*

as sured /ə shûrd′/ *adj.* **1.** self-confident. *An assured manner of speaking gives a person poise.* **2.** guaranteed. *The team thought that its victory in the match was assured.*

as ton ish /ə ston′ ish/ *v.* **astonishes, astonishing, astonished.** to greatly surprise; amaze. *The audience was astonished by the magician's skills.*

as tron o mer /ə stron′ ə mər/ *n.* a scientist who studies heavenly bodies. *Tycho Brahe was a Danish astronomer who built his own observatory.*

a tro cious /ə trō′ shəs/ *adj.* **1.** very bad or unpleasant. *Your table manners are atrocious!* **2.** cruel or wicked. *People imprisoned by the dictator were subject to atrocious conditions.*

B

baf fled /baf′ əld/ *v.* a form of **baffle.** to puzzle greatly or bewilder. *The agents were baffled by the secret messages until they figured out the code.*

bal lot /bal′ ət/ *n.* a secret written vote. *In the voting booth, only the voter can see his or her ballot.*

ban ter /ban′ tər/ *v.* **banters, bantered, bantering.** to make playful jokes. *After the game, we bantered about all the missed shots. n.* playful joking. *There was a lot of friendly banter between the two teams before the basketball game.*

bat tle field /bat′ əl fēld/ *n.* a place where a battle was fought or is being fought. *A famous Civil War battlefield is Bull Run in Virginia.*

bel low /bel′ ō/ *v.* **bellows, bellowing, bellowed.** to make a loud, deep sound. *We heard the bulls bellowing across the pasture. n.* a loud, deep sound. *The hippo let out a bellow of pain as the zookeeper gave him a shot.*

/a/	at
/ā/	late
/â/	care
/ä/	father
/e/	set
/ē/	me
/i/	it
/ī/	kite
/o/	ox
/ō/	rose
/ô/	brought raw
/oi/	coin
/o͝o/	book
/o͞o/	too
/or/	form
/ou/	out
/u/	up
/yo͞o/	cube
/ûr/	turn germ learn firm work
/ə/	about chicken pencil cannon circus
/ch/	chair
/hw/	which
/ng/	ring
/sh/	shop
/th/	thin
/th/	there
/zh/	treasure

be wil der /bi wil′ dər/ *v.* **bewilders, bewildering, bewildered.** to completely confuse or puzzle. *Some people in remote regions of the world would be bewildered by computers.*

bliz zard /bliz′ ərd/ *n.* a heavy snowstorm with strong winds. *The blizzard left two feet of snow on the city streets.*

boom town /büm′ taün′/ *n.* a town that is growing rapidly due to increased business and population. *The discovery of oil in an area would create a boomtown.*

brain wash /brān′ wôsh′, brān′ wosh′/ *v.* **brainwashes, brainwashing, brainwashed.** to change a person's beliefs. *Even your friends might not stand for your brainwashing them into supporting your beliefs.*

budg et /buj′ it/ *n.* a plan that shows an amount of money to be spent for specific purposes in a given period of time. *We created a budget in order to save money for our vacation.*

C

cal cu late /kal′ kyə lāt′/ *v.* **calculates, calculating, calculated. 1.** to figure out in advance; guess. *We calculated that it would take us two hours to reach our destination.* **2.** to figure out using numbers. *Let's calculate how much everyone owes for the pizza.*

car go /kär′ gō/ *n., pl.* **cargoes** or **cargos.** goods carried by ship, plane, or truck. *A large ship can carry many tons of cargo from port to port.*

car pet bag ger /kär′ pit bag′ ər/ *n.* a Northerner who went South to take advantage of the disorder after the Civil War. *Many carpetbaggers were involved in private schemes, but some helped rebuild the economy in the South.*

cav al ry /kav′ əl rē/ *n.* a group of soldiers who fight on horseback. *The cavalry rode down the hill into battle.*

cease /sēs/ *v.* **ceases, ceasing, ceased.** to end, stop. *The snow ceased by evening. The school orchestra will cease performing in May.*

ce les tial /sə les′ chəl/ *adj.* relating to the sky. *Celestial objects include the sun, planets, moons, comets, and other bodies in space.*

chron ic /kron′ ik/ *adj.* **1.** lasting a long time or coming back again and again. *He has a chronic liver disease.* **2.** constant or done by habit. *He is a chronic liar.*

cit i zen ship /sit′ ə zən ship′/ *n.* the position of being a member of a country who enjoys the full rights and duties of that position. *To apply for American citizenship, a person must live legally in the United States for at least five years.*

clar i ty /klar′ i tē/ *n.* the quality of being clear or understandable. *The picture on our new television had amazing clarity. Good writers write with clarity of expression.*

clip per /klip′ ər/ *n.* a fast sailing ship. *American clipper ships of the nineteenth century carried cargo all over the world.*

coarse /kôrs/ *adj.* **1.** thick and rough. *The coarse blankets they gave us at camp made my skin itch.* **2.** made of large parts; not fine. *We walked on coarse sand down to the beach.*

cog /cog/ *n.* one of the teeth on the outer edge of a wheel. *A cog is made to fit between the cogs of another wheel so that when one wheel turns, the other also turns.*

com et /kom′ it/ *n.* a bright heavenly body of ice and dust, with a tail. *A comet's* *tail always points away from the sun.*

com mend /kə mend´/ *v.* **commends, commending, commended.** to praise, recognize; to speak about approvingly. *I must commend you for all your hard work this semester.*

com mod i ty /kə mod´ i tē/ *n., pl.* **commodities.** something that can be bought and sold. *Corn and wheat are agricultural commodities.*

com part ment /kəm pärt´ mənt/ *n.* a division of an enclosed space. *The desk drawers had separate compartments for paper, pens, and paper clips.*

com pas sion /kəm pash´ ən/ *n.* sympathy for another's misfortune; thoughtfulness or pity. *Our neighbor's compassion for poor families led her to give them food and clothing.*

com pli ment /kom´ plə mənt/ *n.* spoken praise; a polite expression of approval. *The teacher's compliments made me blush in front of my classmates.* *v.* **compliments, complimented.** to praise; to pay a compliment. *My aunt complimented me on my spelling skills.*

com ply /kəm plī´/ *v.* **complies, complying, complied.** to agree to follow; to act according to a rule or a request. *I complied with my mother's order to rest until my cold was better.*

com pro mise /kom´ prə miz´/ *n.* the settlement of an argument by agreeing that each side give up something. *The Missouri Compromise admitted both Maine and Missouri as states under different conditions.* *v.* **compromises, compromised.** to reach a settlement by agreeing that each side give up something. *We compromised by deciding to watch both movies Saturday night.*

com rade /kom´ rad/ *n.* a close friend. *My comrade and I hike every Saturday morning.*

con ces sion /kən sesh´ ən/ *n.* **1.** the act of granting or giving in. *My brother made a concession and let me borrow his bicycle.* **2.** permission to operate a business given by a government or other authority. *The town gave our family the concession to sell soft drinks at the summer fair.*

Con fed er ate /kən fed´ ər it/ *n.* a citizen or soldier of the South in the Civil War. *Confederates fought for the eleven southern states that declared themselves a Confederacy separate from the United States.* **confederate.** a person or group joined with another for a common purpose. *The three neighbors were confederates in the fight against crime.*

con fi dence /kon´ fi dens/ *n.* **1.** faith in oneself, assurance. *Confidence will help you do your best.* **2.** trust or faith. *I have confidence in his ability to train the dog.*

con sec u tive /kən sek´ yə tiv/ *adj.* following one after the other without a break. *The high school team won six consecutive games.*

/a/	at
/ā/	late
/â/	care
/ä/	father
/e/	set
/ē/	me
/i/	it
/ī/	kite
/o/	ox
/ō/	rose
/ô/	brought
	raw
/oi/	coin
/o͝o/	book
/o͞o/	too
/or/	form
/ou/	out
/u/	up
/yo͞o/	cube
/ûr/	turn
	germ
	learn
	firm
	work
/ə/	about
	chicken
	pencil
	cannon
	circus
/ch/	chair
/hw/	which
/ng/	ring
/sh/	shop
/th/	thin
/th̶/	there
/zh/	treasure

con spic u ous /kən spik′ ü əs/ *adj.* attracting attention; easily seen. *The pizza sauce left a conspicuous stain on the rug.*

con spir a cy /kən spir′ ə sē/ *n., pl.* **conspiracies.** secret plans made with others to do something wrong. *The members of the group were arrested for conspiracy to rob a bank.*

con stel la tion /kon′ stə lā′ shən/ *n.* a group of stars that seems to form a pattern. *The sky is divided into 88 named constellations.*

con tam i na tion /kən tam′ ə nā′ shən/ *n.* pollution; the act or process of making dirty. *Garbage and other waste dumped into rivers and streams can lead to contamination of the water.*

con tin u al /kən tin′u əl/ *adj.* continuing without a break; continuous. *The continual beat of the drums gave her a headache.*

con tra band /kon′ trə band′/ *n.* goods forbidden by law from being imported or exported. *Boats and ships try to sneak contraband into the United States every day.*

con ven tion /kən ven′ shən/ *n.* a formal meeting for a particular purpose. *We will attend the stamp collection convention.*

co or di nate /kō ôr′ də nāt′/ *v.* **coordinates, coordinating, coordinated.** to work well together; to cause to work together properly. *If we coordinate our efforts, the garage sale will be a success. He is not a good dancer, because he cannot coordinate his body with the music.*

cor por a tion /kôr′ pə rā′ shən/ *n.* a group of people with legal power to act as one person. *A corporation has the right to enter into contracts and buy and sell property.*

cor ral /kə ral′/ *n.* a fenced pen for cattle, horses, or other animals. *A corral keeps farm animals from wandering.*

coun sel /koun′ səl/ *n.* **1.** advice or opinions. *My friends give me counsel when I ask for it.* **2.** a lawyer who gives legal advice. *John Dean was counsel for President Richard M. Nixon.* *v.* **counsels, counseling, counseled.** to advise. *My friends counseled me to go to college.*

cra ter /krā′ tər/ *n.* a large hole in the ground. *Earth's moon is covered with craters of all sizes.*

cun ning /kun′ ing/ *adj.* clever at fooling others; tricky. *The cunning hyena often hunts in packs at night or even during the daytime.*

cur rent /kûr′ ənt/ *n.* **1.** a flow of electricity. *Never touch a downed power line, because electric current flowing through the wires might cause you serious harm.* **2.** a part of air or water that is moving along a path. *A strong current carried our canoe down the river. adj.* belonging to the present. *I try to stay informed about current events.*

D

dead lock /ded′ lok′/ *n.* a standstill; situation where no progress can be made. *After one month, the deadlock between the workers and the company was broken.* *v.* **deadlocks, deadlocked.** to come to a standstill. *The two sides deadlocked over the issue of wages.*

dec ade /dek′ ād/ *n.* a time span of ten years. *The sixties are a decade known for social turmoil in the United States.*

de ceased /di sēst′/ *adj.* dead. *Our school is named after a deceased U.S. president.*

de ceive /di sēv´/ *v.* **deceives, deceiving, deceived.** to lie or mislead. *I deceived my sister by telling her there were no more cookies.*

de fi cien cy /di fish´ ən cē/ *n., pl.* **deficiencies.** a lack or a shortage of something. *The vitamin C deficiency called scurvy was first identified in sailors on long sea voyages.*

de ject ed /di jek´ tid/ *adj.* sad or depressed. *The soccer players were very dejected after they lost the game.*

de lec ta ble /di lek´ tə bəl/ *adj.* very pleasing or delicious. *We were served a tray of delectable sweets after our meal.*

del e ga tion /del´ i gā´ shən/ *n.* a group of representatives. *A delegation of students went to the principal's office to state their concerns.*

de part ment /di pärt´ mənt/ *n.* a separate division of an organization. *The children's department is in the back of the bookstore.*

dep u ty /dep´ yə tē/ *n., pl.* **deputies.** a person appointed to act for another person. *A sheriff may appoint deputies as needed to help with enforcing the law.*

des ig nate /dez´ ig nāt´/ *v.* **designates, designating, designated. 1.** to name to a position; to appoint. *The actress was designated grand marshal of the parade.* **2.** to show or point out. *The color blue designates lakes and other bodies of water on many maps and globes.*

des ti ny /des´ tə nē/ *n.* the events that happen to a person; fate. *I felt that it was my destiny to follow in my father's footsteps and become a firefighter.*

di ag no sis /dī´ əg nō´ sis/ *n.* **1.** the act or process of identifying a disease. *The scientist's diagnosis showed that the disease had spread.* **2.** the conclusion reached by careful examination. *The plumber's diagnosis was that we had a broken pipe.*

di a grams /dī´ ə gramz´/ *pl. n.* drawings showing plans of how things work. *We studied the diagrams before we tried to assemble the bookcase.*

die sel /dē´ zəl/ *n.* a special type of engine. *Fuel oil in a diesel engine burns by heat produced by air compression in the engine.*

di lem ma /di lem´ ə/ *n.* a situation requiring a difficult choice. *My most difficult dilemma was whether to use a crutch or a cane after my accident.*

din /din/ *n.* a loud, continuous noise. *The din from the kitchen kept us from enjoying our meal in the restaurant.*

dis as ter /di zas´ tər/ *n.* **1.** a sudden misfortune. *The flood was a disaster for the small town.* **2.** something that fails or doesn't go right. *High winds turned the tent party into a disaster.*

/a/	at
/ā/	late
/â/	care
/ä/	father
/e/	set
/ē/	me
/i/	it
/ī/	kite
/o/	ox
/ō/	rose
/ô/	brought
	raw
/oi/	coin
/o͝o/	book
/o͞o/	too
/or/	form
/ou/	out
/u/	up
/yo͞o/	cube
/ûr/	turn
	germ
	learn
	firm
	work
/ə/	about
	chicken
	pencil
	cannon
	circus
/ch/	chair
/hw/	which
/ng/	ring
/sh/	shop
/th/	thin
/ŧħ/	there
/zh/	treasure

dis charge /dis´ chärj/ *n.* dismissal from service or a job. *The soldier received his discharge from the army after the war ended.* /dis chärj´/ *v.* **discharges, discharging, discharged. 1.** to shoot or send forth. *Men dressed in Civil War uniforms discharged the cannons at the fort during the ceremony.* **2.** to send or let out. *The factory was fined for discharging waste into the river.*

dis miss /dis mis´/ *v.* **dismisses, dismissing, dismissed. 1.** to send away or allow to leave. *The teacher dismissed the class early on the last day of school.* **2.** to take away the job of; to fire. *The worker was dismissed because he was caught stealing.* **3.** to put aside from consideration. *We dismissed the rumor as untrue.*

dis rupt /dis rupt´/ *v.* **disrupts, disrupting, disrupted.** to upset or break up. *A dog ran out on the playing field and disrupted the baseball game.*

dis trict /dis ´ trikt/ *n.* a division of a city, state, country, or other area. *Some state taxes are used to support the school districts in the state.*

do main /dō mān´/ *n.* **1.** the land owned or controlled by a person or a government. *The land the state university occupies is public domain.* **2.** a field of interest or knowledge. *Planets and galaxies fall within the domain of astronomy.*

dom i nate /dom´ ə nāt/ *v.* **dominates, dominating, dominated. 1.** to control or be the main influence on. *Fear dominated our town as the hurricane approached.* **2.** to have the chief position in or over something. *The Space Needle dominates Seattle's skyline.*

drought /drout/ *n.* a long period of no rain or very little rain. *Farms in the Midwest suffered severely during the drought.*

E

ea ger /ē´ gər/ *adj.* **1.** showing great interest in something. *The children at the zoo had eager looks on their faces.* **2.** wanting very much to do something. *We were eager to go to summer camp.*

ee rie /ir´ ē/ *adj.* weird and frightening. *With only the moon's eerie glow to light the country road, we walked quickly home.*

e lat ed /i lā´ tid/ *adj.* joyful; in high spirits. *The elated children jumped and shouted when the snowstorm closed school for the day.*

eld er ly /el´ dər lē/ *adj.* rather old. *My elderly aunt is very active in our community.*

e lim i na tion /i lim´ ə nā´ shən/ *n.* removal. *The elimination of complaints was the store manager's goal.*

e lite /i lēt´/ *n.* the best or finest members. *Many of our city's elite were invited to the political celebration.*

e man ci pa tion /i man´ sə pā´ shən/ *n.* the act of setting free from slavery or control. *The Emancipation Proclamation freed the slaves.*

e mit /i mit ´/ *v.* **emits, emitting, emitted.** to give off or send forth. *Stars emit heat and light.*

en force ment /en fors´ mənt/ *n.* the act of making sure that laws are obeyed. *The candidate supported strong law enforcement.*

en list /en list´/ *v.* **enlists, enlisting, enlisted. 1.** to join a group or cause. *Both my brothers enlisted in the army after high school.* **2.** to get for a group or project. *How many students do you think we can we enlist for our recycling drive?*

en ter prise /en´ tər prīz´/ *n.* a project or an undertaking. *An* *enterprise is often something that is important or difficult to do.*

ep i dem ic /ep´ i dem´ ik/ *n.* the rapid spread of a disease. *An epidemic occurs when a disease spreads quickly among many people in an area.*

e ter nal /i tûr´ nəl/ *adj.* **1.** without beginning or end. *The beauty of outer space is eternal.* **2.** seeming to last forever. *We complained about the eternal noise of our neighbor's stereo system.*

e ven hand ed /ē´ vən han´ ded/ *adj.* fair; just. *The evenhanded umpire called a strike and stuck to his decision.*

ex cep tion al /ek sep´ shə nəl/ *adj.* very unusual; out of the ordinary. *The young singer has exceptional talent.*

ex claim /ek sklām´/ *v.* **exclaims, exclaimed, exclaiming.** to speak or shout suddenly or with force; to express surprise. *"You borrowed my jacket without asking me first!" exclaimed my brother.*

ex clu sive /ek sklōō´ siv/ *adj.* **1.** open only to a certain group of people. *The exclusive resort was for members only.* **2.** being the only one of its kind. *The reporter got an exclusive interview with the senator.*

ex cur sion /ek skûr´ zhən/ *n.* **1.** a short trip made for pleasure or for a special reason. *The excursion to Catalina Island was very enjoyable.* **2.** a round trip at a reduced fare, as on a plane or train. *We went on a weekend excursion to Chicago.*

ex e cute /ek´ si kūt´/ *v.* **executes, executing, executed.** to carry out or enforce. *Army privates must execute the orders they receive from their sergeants.*

ex ec u tive /eg zek´ yə tiv/ *n.* **1.** a person who manages a business. *A president and vice president are executives of a company.* **2.** the branch of government concerned with carrying out the laws of a nation. *The president heads the executive branch of the United States government.*

ex ot ic /eg zot´ ik/ *adj.* foreign or strangely beautiful or unusual. *These exotic blue butterflies are found only in South America.*

ex pe di tion /ek´ spi dish´ ən/ *n.* a journey made for a particular purpose. *A group of scientists made an expedition to the south pole to perform experiments.*

ex port /ek´ spôrt´ / *n.* something that is sold or traded to another country. *Automobiles are an export of Japan and the United Kingdom.* /ek spôrt´/ *v.* **exports, exporting, exported.** to send goods to other countries to be sold or traded. *The United States exports wheat to other countries.*

ex quis ite /ek skwiz´ it/ *adj.* of great beauty or perfection. *The Art Institute of Chicago has many exquisite works of art.*

/a/	at
/ā/	late
/â/	care
/ä/	father
/e/	set
/ē/	me
/i/	it
/ī/	kite
/o/	ox
/ō/	rose
/ô/	brought
	raw
/oi/	coin
/o͞o/	book
/ōō/	too
/or/	form
/ou/	out
/u/	up
/yōō/	cube
/ûr/	turn
	germ
	learn
	firm
	work
/ə/	about
	chicken
	pencil
	cannon
	circus
/ch/	chair
/hw/	which
/ng/	ring
/sh/	shop
/th/	thin
/ th/	there
/zh/	treasure

F

fi nan cial /fi nan′ shəl/ *adj.* relating to money matters. *Banks handle the financial affairs of individuals, companies, and nations.*

flaw /flô/ *n.* a scratch or other defect. *The large china plate had a small flaw. v.* to make defective. *The large crack flawed the vase.*

flu ent /flu′ ənt/ *adj.* **1.** spoken or written smoothly. *The fluent poetry of Poe is fun to read aloud.* **2.** able to speak or write smoothly. *My sister is fluent in Russian and French.*

flur ry /flûr′ ē/ *n., pl.* **flurries. 1.** a brief, light snowfall. *On my way to school, I hoped that the flurries would turn into heavy snow.* **2.** a sudden outburst. *There is a flurry of activity every morning when my family awakens.*

foe /fō/ *n.* enemy. *Tennyson wrote, "He makes no friend who never made a foe."*

for eign er /for′ ə nər/ *n.* a person not native to a country. *We were surprised to find ourselves looked upon as foreigners when we were in France.*

fore sight /for′ sīt′/ *n.* looking or thinking ahead. *The travelers showed foresight in bringing food and water for the long drive.*

for ty-nin er / for′ tē nī′ nər/ *n.* a person who went to California in 1849 looking for gold. *The forty-niners arrived in California full of hopes and dreams.*

fo rum /for′ əm/ *n.* a public meeting about problems or issues. *The school held an open forum to discuss the recent destruction of school property.*

frail /frāl/ *adj.* lacking in strength. *My great-grandmother is becoming frail as she gets older.*

fran tic /fran′ tik/ *adj.* wildly excited by worry or fear. *I became frantic when I couldn't find my wallet.*

frig id /frij′ id/ *adj.* freezing cold. *Both the north pole and the south pole have frigid climates.*

front /frunt/ *n.* **1.** the border between two air masses of different temperatures. *The weather forecaster predicted a drop in temperatures when the cold front moved into the area.* **2.** the part that comes first or that faces forward. *The table of contents is at the front of the book.*

G

gal ley /gal′ ē/ *n., pl.* **galleys.** the kitchen in a ship or an airplane. *The smell of baked chicken came from the galley of the plane.*

gauge /gāj/ *n.* **1.** a measuring tool. *An air pressure gauge measures the amount of air in a tire.* **2.** a standard measure. *Many of the world's railroads run on standard gauge rails 1.4 meters apart. v.* to measure. *Scientists can gauge the speed of a tornado.*

gear /gir/ *n.* **1.** a wheel in a machine with teeth on the edge. *The teeth on a gear cause another gear to turn.* **2.** an arrangement of such wheels used to change movements. *I put my bike in low gear to climb the hill.* **3.** equipment used for a special purpose. *We packed our football gear in the van.*

gen er a tor /jen′ ə rā′ tər/ *n.* a machine that makes energy. *A generator produces steam, electricity, or other forms of energy.*

ge net ic /jə net′ ik/ *adj.* relating to inherited traits; hereditary. *My father told me that his flat feet are the result of genetic traits.*

gra cious /grā′ shəs/ *adj.* kind and polite; full of charm. *The gracious hostess* *made each guest at the party feel special.*

grad u a tion /grăj′ ū ā′ shən/ *n.*
1. the act or process of finishing a course of study. *Graduation from primary school may come after the sixth grade.* 2. the ceremony of graduating from a school or college. *The president was the speaker at the university's graduation ceremony.*

grat ing /grā′ ting/ *adj.* making a harsh, irritating sound. *The rim of the flat tire made a grating noise as we stopped by the side of the road.*

griev ance /grē′ vəns/ *n., pl.* **grievances.** a wrong that causes unhappiness. *The community's list of grievances included potholes in many roads.*

H

half-mast /hăf′ măst′/ *n.* down to the middle. *Flags around the world were flown at half-mast when the princess died.*

haugh ty /hô′ tē/ *adj.* overly proud; thinking of oneself as much better than others. *The haughty actress refused to speak to fans or reporters.*

hor i zon tal /hor′ ə zon′ təl/ *adj.* parallel to level ground; flat and straight across. *I drew a horizontal line on the map.*

hunch /hunch/ *n.* a feeling or guess. *I have a hunch that the telephone is about to ring.* v. **hunches, hunching, hunched.** to draw up or raise. *We hunched our shoulders against the wind.*

I

il lu sion /i lōō′ zhən/ *n.* a misleading idea. *Before I traveled, I had the illusion that life abroad was exactly the same as life in the United States.*

im mune /i myōōn′/ *adj.*
1. protected from a disease. *We received vaccinations at school to make us immune to measles.*
2. safe from or free from something. *A politician should be immune from corruption.*

im pair /im pâr′/ *v.* **impairs, impairing, impaired.** to damage or weaken. *Illness impaired the horse's strength.*

im ped i ment /im ped′ ə mənt/ *n.*
1. something that slows or stops progress. *The speed bump was an impediment for drivers.*
2. a physical fault. *A speech impediment did not stop the student from doing well in school.*

im port /im′ port/ *n.* something that is brought in from another country for sale or use. *Tea is an import from India.* /im port′/ *v.* **imports, importing, imported.** to bring in goods from another country for sale or use. *The United States imports coffee from Brazil.*

im pose /im pōz′/ *v.* **imposes, imposing, imposed.** to force or demand. *The teacher imposed his rules on the class.*

in def i nite /in def′ ə nit/ *adj.*
1. not certain, not exact. *My plans for college are still indefinite.* 2. having no limits. *I will have to wear this cast on my arm for an indefinite number of weeks.*

/a/	at
/ā/	late
/â/	care
/ä/	father
/e/	set
/ē/	me
/i/	it
/ī/	kite
/o/	ox
/ō/	rose
/ô/	brought
	raw
/oi/	coin
/o͝o/	book
/o͞o/	too
/or/	form
/ou/	out
/u/	up
/yo͞o/	cube
/ûr/	turn
	germ
	learn
	firm
	work
/ə/	about
	chicken
	pencil
	cannon
	circus
/ch/	chair
/hw/	which
/ng/	ring
/sh/	shop
/th/	thin
/ᵺ/	there
/zh/	treasure

in fan cy /in′ fən sē/ *n.* **1.** the condition or period of being a baby. *People and animals depend on their parents during infancy.* **2.** the earliest period in the development of something. *When the train was in its infancy, steam power was used for the engines.*

in her i tance /in her′ i təns/ *n.* something that is passed down from one's parents or relatives. *My inheritance from my grandfather included a large desk and some books.*

in quire /in kwīr′/ *v.* **inquires, inquiring, inquired.** to ask, to seek information. *We stopped twice to inquire about the location of the historic landmark.*

in scrip tion /in skrip′ shən/ *n.* symbols, letters, or words written or carved on something. *The inscription on the old coin showed a two-headed eagle.*

in se cu ri ty /in′ si kyoor′ i tē/ *n., pl.* **insecurities.** lack of self-confidence; self-doubt. *When someone is rude, it is sometimes because of his or her insecurity.*

in sig ni a /in sig′ nē ə/ *n.* a badge or other mark showing a person's rank or position; a symbol. *The firefighter wore his insignia on his uniform.*

in spir a tion /in′ spə rā′ shən/ *n.* **1.** a good influence. *Helen Keller served as an inspiration for many people.* **2.** stirring the mind or imagination. *Native American life gave inspiration to photographer Edward Curtis.*

in sult /in′ sult/ *n.* a rude remark. *In the eighteenth and nineteenth centuries, insults sometimes resulted in duels.* /in sult′/ *v.* **insults, insulted, insulting.** to speak or treat in a rude way. *When you doubt my honesty, you insult me.*

in te grate /in′ ti grāt′/ *v.* **integrates, integrating, integrated. 1.** to bring parts together into a whole. *The student had to integrate his notes from several books into a report about the American South.* **2.** to make open to people of all races. *Some schools waited until they were forced to integrate.*

in teg ri ty /in teg′ ri tē/ *n.* complete honesty; honor. *A person who hides the truth has little integrity.*

in ten tion /in ten′ shən/ *n.* purpose or plan. *The mayor had good intentions, but the city council often did not support him.*

in ter lude /in′ tər lood′/ *n.* the period of time between events. *There was a brief interlude between the musical numbers in the concert.*

in ter mis sion /in′ tər mish′ ən/ *n.* a pause or rest between events. *The movie was so long that there was a ten-minute intermission in the middle.*

in ter val /in′ tər vəl/ *n.* time or space between. *There were intervals of 15 minutes between the acts of the play.*

in ter ven tion /in′ tər ven′ shən/ *n.* the act of coming between opposing sides. *The referee's intervention stopped a fight on the soccer field.*

in tim i date /in tim′ i dāt/ *v.* **intimidates, intimidating, intimidated. 1.** to make fearful; to frighten. *Young children are often intimidated by large dogs.* **2.** to influence by threats or violence. *The bully tried to intimidate the children in the school yard.*

in trep id /in trep′ id/ *adj.* brave and bearing up under difficulty; fearless. *The intrepid climbers made their way to the top of Mt. Everest.*

in va sion /in vā′ zhen/ *n.* **1.** the entrance of an armed force, as into a country, in order to conquer. *The army was prepared for an invasion by enemy* forces. **2.** an intrusion or violation; infringement. *Reading my diary is an invasion of privacy.*

in ven to ry /in′ vən tor′ ē/ *n., pl.* **inventories. 1.** a detailed list of goods in stock. *We helped our favorite store take inventory at the end of the year.* **2.** the articles on such a list. *The store has a large inventory of women's shoes and clothing.*

J

ju ve nile /jōō′ və nəl/ *n.* a young person. *Clothing for juveniles is on the second floor of the store.* *adj.* **1.** of or for children and young people. *There are many good juvenile authors whose books are in our library.* **2.** childish. *Her juvenile behavior embarrassed the whole family.*

L

land own er /land′ ō′ nər/ *n.* a person who owns land. *Landowners in the South built huge plantations before the Civil War.*

le ver /le′ vər/ *n.* **1.** a rod or bar for lifting or prying things open. *A lever can help a person lift a stack of heavy boxes.* **2.** a handle used to operate a machine. *The operator used a lever to lower the front of the snowplow.*

lin e ar /lin′ ē ər/ *adj.* **1.** relating to lines. *The teacher made a linear drawing to illustrate geometric figures.* **2.** relating to length. *Meters and kilometers are linear measurements.*

lu min ous /lōō′ mə nəs/ *adj.* bright and shining. *The luminous glow of dozens of fireflies could be seen from the porch of the cabin.*

M

ma ter ni ty /mə tûr′ ni tē/ *n.* motherhood; the state of being a mother. *Our dog's maternity has changed her behavior.*

mat ri mo ny /mat′ rə mō′ nē/ *n.* marriage; the state of being married. *Matrimony is a serious step to take in life.*

mes sen ger /mes′ ən jər/ *n.* a person who brings news or runs errands. *Some messengers use bicycles to deliver important mail to businesses in cities.*

me te or /mē′ tē ər/ *n.* Space matter that burns as it falls to Earth. *The streaks of light in the night sky were meteors.*

mis sion /mish′ ən/ *n.* **1.** an assigned task or service. *The scientist thought her mission in life was to find cures for serious diseases.* **2.** a group of people sent somewhere to do a special job. *Firefighters were on a mission to help put out the forest fire.* **3.** a church or other place where missionaries work. *The Alamo was an early Spanish mission in Texas.*

mo bile /mō bēl′/ *n.* a kind of sculpture with movable parts that hangs on wires or rods. *Alexander Calder is famous for his clever mobiles.* /mō′ bəl/ *adj.* able to move or be moved. *My grandparents live in a mobile home and travel around the country.*

/a/	at
/ā/	late
/â/	care
/ä/	father
/e/	set
/ē/	me
/i/	it
/ī/	kite
/o/	ox
/ō/	rose
/ô/	brought raw
/oi/	coin
/ŏŏ/	book
/ōō/	too
/or/	form
/ou/	out
/u/	up
/yōō/	cube
/ûr/	turn germ learn firm work
/ə/	about chicken pencil cannon circus
/ch/	chair
/hw/	which
/ng/	ring
/sh/	shop
/th/	thin
/th/	there
/zh/	treasure

mo tive /mō′ tiv/ *n.* the reason that a person does something. *Buying a new computer is a strong motive for getting a summer job.*

mur mur /mûr′ mər/ *n.* a low, soft sound. *The murmur of the brook was a pleasant background to our picnic lunch.* *v.* **murmurs, murmured, murmuring.** to make or say with a low, soft sound. *Please murmur at the movies.*

N

nav i ga tion /nav′ i gā′ shən/ *n.* the act of guiding a ship or an aircraft. *At night, the positions of the stars can help in the navigation of a ship.*

no mad /nō′ mad/ *n.* **1.** a member of a group or tribe that does not have a permanent home. *Gypsies are a group of nomads who came from India and now live mainly in Europe.* **2.** a wanderer who has no permanent home. *A circus performer may live like a nomad for months at a time.*

no ta ble /nō′ tə bəl/ *adj.* worthy of notice; important. *Thomas Edison had notable success with his inventions.*

nour ish ment /nûr′ ish mənt/ *n.* something that promotes health and growth. *Growing plants need proper nourishment.*

nui sance /noo′ səns/ *n.* a pest; something or someone that annoys or offends. *Trying to walk on a street without sidewalks is a nuisance.*

O

ob struct /əb strukt′/ *v.* **obstructs, obstructing, obstructed.** to block or prevent passage. *Rock slides obstructed the scenic highway.*

ob vi ous /ob′ vē əs/ *adj.* easily seen or understood. *The obvious solution was to leave the cat at home.*

o mit /ō mit′/ *v.* **omitted, omitting.** to leave out; fail to include. *I will omit her name from the list because she is unable to attend the party.*

out look /out′ look′/ *n.* **1.** a point of view. *A positive outlook helps one through the day.* **2.** a view into the future. *The outlook for the economy in our city is very good.*

out ra geous /out rā′ jəs/ *adj.* shocking; going beyond proper limits. *The behavior of the fans after the soccer match was outrageous.*

o ver whelm /ō′ vər welm′/ *v.* **1.** to overcome completely; overpower or crush. *The enemy forces overwhelmed the guards.* **2.** to cover or bury completely. *The darkness overwhelmed the neighborhood.*

P

par a sites /par′ ə sīts′/ *pl. n.* organisms that live in or on other organisms. *Fleas are parasites on cats and dogs.*

pa ter ni ty /pə tûr′ ni tē/ *n.* fatherhood; the state of being a father. *Paternity brings responsibilities for the present and the future.*

per cep tion /pər sep′ shən/ *n.* awareness; observation. *Events confirmed our perception that the scientist had been treated unfairly.*

per il /per′ əl/ *n.* **1.** danger; a chance of risk or harm. *A police officer's life is sometimes in peril.* **2.** something dangerous. *Snakes and sweltering heat are perils faced by desert travelers.*

per se cute /pûr′ si koot′/ *v.* **persecutes, persecuting, persecuted.** to continually treat a person or a group cruelly or unfairly. *Many immigrants to the United States suffered persecution in their native countries.*

phe nom e non /fə nom′ ə non′/ *n.*, *pl.* **phenomena. 1.** an extraordinary thing or person. *Beethoven was a phenomenon of music composition.* **2.** an event or fact that can be seen or sensed. *The phenomenon of the northern lights has delighted humans for many years.*

plead /plēd/ *v.* **pleads, pleaded** or **pled, pleading.** to beg. *My dog pleads to go for a walk.*

poise /poiz/ *n.* a calm and assured manner. *We were all surprised by my sister's poise when she addressed the student body.*

pol i ti cian /pol′ i tish′ ən/ *n.* a person who runs for office. *The president is one of four politicians in his family.*

polls /pōlz/ *pl. n.* the place where votes are cast. *More voters go to the polls for a presidential election.*

pos ses sions /pə zesh′ enz/ *n.* things that are held or owned. *Some of her possessions are valuable antiques.*

pre cip i ta tion /pri sip′ i tā′ shən/ *n.* water falling in the form of rain, snow, sleet, or hail. *The amount of precipitation is lower in the summer than in the winter.*

pre oc cu pied /prē ok′ yə pīd′/ *adj.* lost in thought. *My father doesn't hear me when he is preoccupied with the newspaper.*

prime /prīm/ *adj.* **1.** of the best quality; excellent. *Meat in the* grocery store marked "prime" is the highest grade of meat. **2.** first or greatest in importance or value. *The mayor's prime concern is the quality of education in the schools.*

pri or /prī′ ər/ *adj.* earlier, before in time or order. *His prior appointment with a tutor kept him from watching the beginning of the game.*

pro ceeds /prō′ sēdz/ *pl. n.* money raised for a special purpose by selling something; profits. *The book club used the proceeds from the used-book sale to help the needy.*

pro hib it /prō hib′ it/ *v.* **prohibits, prohibited. 1.** to forbid by authority. *Speaking in a loud voice is prohibited in the library.* **2.** to prevent or stop. *Poor eyesight prohibits my grandmother from driving.*

pro long /prə lông′/ *v.* **prolongs, prolonging, prolonged.** to extend in time. *Radio serials prolonged the suspense of a mystery story from week to week.*

prop a gan da /prop′ ə gan′ də/ *n.* beliefs spread to gain supporters. *Propaganda can be untrue or unfairly presented.*

pro pose /prō prōz′/ *v.* **proposes, proposed, proposing. 1.** to suggest or put forward for discussion or consideration. *To everyone's relief, the two presidents proposed a new peace agreement.* **2.** to intend or plan to do something. *What do you propose to do about your failing grades?*

/a/	at
/ā/	late
/â/	care
/ä/	father
/e/	set
/ē/	me
/i/	it
/ī/	kite
/o/	ox
/ō/	rose
/ô/	brought
	raw
/oi/	coin
/o͝o/	book
/o͞o/	too
/or/	form
/ou/	out
/u/	up
/yo͞o/	cube
/ûr/	turn
	germ
	learn
	firm
	work
/ə/	about
	chicken
	pencil
	cannon
	circus
/ch/	chair
/hw/	which
/ng/	ring
/sh/	shop
/th/	thin
/ th/	there
/zh/	treasure

pro voke /prə vōk´/ *v.* **provokes, provoking, provoked. 1.** to make angry. *Please don't provoke me.* **2.** to bring out. *The newspaper article about school taxes provoked discussion.*

pub lic ly /pub´ li klē/ *adv.* in a manner open to all. *The governor publicly announced his plans not to seek another term in office.*

pul ley /pŏŏl´ ē/ *n., pl.* **pulleys.** a wheel with a groove around it that a chain or rope can be pulled over. *A pulley is used to lift heavy objects.*

pur sue /pər sōō´/ *v.* **1.** to strive for; seek. *After high school, she will pursue a college degree.* **2.** to follow in order to overtake or capture. *The hounds will pursue the fox until they catch it.*

R

re cep tive /ri sep´ tiv/ *adj.* open to new ideas or suggestions. *My parents were receptive to my trying out for the school play.*

rec og nize /rek´ əg nīz´/ *v.* **recognizes, recognizing, recognized. 1.** to know as someone seen or known before. *I recognized my cousin's face easily even after ten years.* **2.** to be aware of; to understand clearly. *We recognized our duty to report the traffic accident.*

re deem /ri dēm´/ *v.* **redeems, redeeming, redeemed. 1.** to exchange something for money, a prize, or merchandise. *We can redeem this coupon for a free drink.* **2.** to make up for. *The team redeemed its poor showing in the first half by scoring two touchdowns in the second half of the game.*

red o lent /red´ ə lənt/ *adj.* giving off a pleasant odor. *The air in the kitchen was redolent with the smell of bread baking in the oven.*

re gret /ri gret´/ *n.* a feeling of sadness or sorrow. *We had no regrets about moving to California.* *v.* **regrets, regretting, regretted.** to feel sorry about. *I regretted my angry words to my sister.*

re sem ble /ri zem´ bəl/ *v.* **resembles, resembling, resembled.** to be similar to. *Your new coat resembles mine.*

re sign /rē zīn´/ *v.* **resigns, resigning, resigned.** to give up a job or position. *My mother resigned her job when we moved to another city.*

re sound ing /ri zound´ ing/ *adj.* full of loud, echoing sound. *The concert hall, resounding with beautiful music, was filled with appreciative applause.*

rev o lu tion /rev´ ə lōō´ shən/ *n.* **1.** the overthrow of an existing government and the setting up of a new system. *The Russian Revolution took place in 1917.* **2.** a sudden or complete change. *The Industrial Revolution began in England in the eighteenth century.*

re volve /ri volv´/ *v.* **revolves, revolving, revolved. 1.** to move in a circle around something else. *There are 39 moons revolving around the planet Jupiter.* **2.** to spin around a central point. *A car's wheels revolve when the car is moving.*

rig ging /rig´ ing/ *n.* the ropes that support the sails of a ship. *Rigging includes all the ropes, wires, and chains used on a sailing ship.*

S

sat el lite /sat´ ə līt´/ *n.* an object that goes around another. *Satellites can be natural, like Earth's moon, or human-made, such as weather satellites.*

scald ing /skôld´ ing/ *adj.* almost boiling hot. *The workers were burned by the scalding water from the pipes.*

scarce /skârs/ *adj.* difficult to get or find. *Modern conveniences are scarce in some parts of Africa.*

se cede /si sēd′/ *v.* **secedes, seceding, seceded.** to formally withdraw from an organization or group. *President Lincoln did not want any Southern states to secede from the Union.*

se cre cy /sē′ krə sē/ *n.* state of keeping something from general knowledge. *The thieves made their plans in secrecy.*

seg re ga tion /seg′ ri gā′ shən/ *n.* the separation of individuals or groups; the separation of people by race. *The Civil Rights Act of 1964 helped end segregation in education.*

ship shape /ship′ shāp′/ *adj.* in good or proper order. *Keeping your room in shipshape condition means keeping it neat.*

shrewd /shrood/ *adj.* clever, especially in practical matters. *The shrewd shopper found many bargains at the mall.*

shrill /shril/ *adj.* sharp and high-pitched in sound. *The referee's shrill whistle could hardly be heard above the roar of the crowd in the stadium.*

sieve /siv/ *n.* a metal utensil that has many holes in the bottom. *A sieve may be used for draining or for sifting.*

spec trum /spek′ trəm/ *n.* the band of colors into which white light is separated. *The colors of the spectrum always appear in the order of red, orange, yellow, green, blue, indigo, and violet.*

stake /stāk/ *n.* a sharp, pointed stick. *A stake is pointed at one end so that it can be driven into the ground.* *v.* **staking, staked.** **1.** to hold or fasten with a stake. *I helped my mother stake the tomato plants in the garden.* **2.** to mark with a stake. *The forty-niners rushed to stake their claims.*

stam pede /stam pēd′/ *n.* **1.** a sudden rush of frightened animals. *A wolf approached the herd of cows and caused a stampede.* **2.** a sudden rush of a lot of people. *When the doors of the store opened early for the big sale, there was a stampede.* *v.* to make a wild rush. *The cattle stampeded when the thunder and lightning started.*

ster ile /ster′ əl/ *adj.* free from bacteria and dirt. *Sterile bandages are used to protect cuts and wounds from dirt.*

stren u ous /stren′ yoo əs/ *adj.* requiring great effort. *Cowboys working on a large ranch must perform very strenuous tasks.*

struc ture /struk′ chər/ *n.* **1.** the way in which something is organized or arranged. *The structure of a cell is of interest to biologists.* **2.** anything built. *A school, a house, a bridge, or a building is a structure.*

sub dued /səb dood′/ *adj.* lacking energy or strength. *The class was very subdued after hearing the sad news.* *v.* a form of **subdue.** to control or overcome. *The zookeeper subdued the angry ape.*

/a/	at
/ā/	late
/â/	care
/ä/	father
/e/	set
/ē/	me
/i/	it
/ī/	kite
/o/	ox
/ō/	rose
/ô/	brought
	raw
/oi/	coin
/oo/	book
/ōō/	too
/or/	form
/ou/	out
/u/	up
/yoo/	cube
/ûr/	turn
	germ
	learn
	firm
	work
/ə/	about
	chicken
	pencil
	cannon
	circus
/ch/	chair
/hw/	which
/ng/	ring
/sh/	shop
/th/	thin
/th/	there
/zh/	treasure

sub mar ine /sub′ mə rēn′/ *n.* a ship that can travel under water. *Some submarines are used to research ocean life.* *adj.* growing or lying beneath the surface of the sea. *Submarine plants include various kinds of seaweed.*

sub or di nate /sə bôr′ də nit/ *adj.* lower in rank. *A captain is subordinate to a major.*

sub side /səb sīd′/ *v.* **subsides, subsiding, subsided. 1.** to lessen. *My fear subsided when I got used to swimming under water.* **2.** to sink to a lower level. *The water from the flood finally subsided after three days.*

sub ter ra ne an /sub′ tə rā′ nē ən/ *adj.* beneath Earth's surface. *Cars and trucks turned on their lights when they went through the subterranean passage.*

suf frage /suf′ rij/ *n.* the right to vote. *The nineteenth amendment to the United States Constitution granted suffrage to women.*

sum mon /sum′ ən/ *v.* **summons, summoning, summoned. 1.** to send for. *The day after my rude remark in class, I was summoned to the principal's office.* **2.** to stir or gather. *We summoned our courage and asked for the actor's autograph.*

su per fi cial /sōō′ pər fish′ əl/ *adj.* **1.** relating to or being located on the surface. *Our cat's wounds were only superficial.* **2.** shallow; lacking depth of thought. *My friend's interest in movie stars seems superficial to me.*

su per hu man /sōō′ pər hōō′ mən/ *adj.* far beyond normal human ability. *Weight lifters seem to have superhuman strength.*

su per sede /sōō′ pər sēd′/ *v.* **supersedes, superseding, superseded.** to take the place of. *Computers have superseded typewriters in homes and businesses.*

su per vi sor /sōō′ pər vī′ zər/ *n.* one with authority who oversees. *The supervisor in the department store directs ten salesclerks.*

sus pect /sus′ pekt′/ *n.* someone believed to have committed a crime. *The suspect ran for ten blocks before he was caught by the police.* /sə spekt′/ *v.* **suspects, suspecting, suspected. 1.** to suppose something to be true. *I suspect that other celestial objects will be discovered.* **2.** to think someone guilty without proof. *The police suspected a store employee of the theft.*

sus pense /sə spens′/ *n.* the state of being undecided, worried, and in doubt. *The exciting movie kept me in suspense.*

swear /swâr/ *v.* **swearing, swore, sworn.** to make a solemn promise. *I swore to my parents that I would always tell the truth.*

swel ter ing /swel′ tər ing/ *adj.* very hot. *We postponed our picnic because of the sweltering weather.*

⊤ ▬▬▬▬▬▬▬▬▬▬▬▬▬▬▬▬▬

te di ous /tē′ dē əs/ *adj.* boring; causing weariness because of length or dullness. *We had a very tedious wait at the airport.*

tep id /tep′ id/ *adj.* slightly warm. *I had talked on the telephone so long that my bathwater was tepid.*

ther mo stat /thûr′ mə stat′/ *n.* an instrument that automatically controls temperature. *Ovens, cars, and the furnaces in buildings have thermostats.*

thwart /thwort/ *v.* **thwarts, thwarting, thwarted.** to prevent from doing something. *Our efforts to cross the river were thwarted by the rapid current.*

time-hon ored /tīm′ on′ ərd/ *adj.* respected for age or usage. *Giving someone a gift on his or her birthday is a time-honored custom.*

tol er ate /tol′ ə rāt′/ *v.* **tolerates, tolerated, tolerating. 1.** to accept or allow. *Shouting in the library is not tolerated.* **2.** to put up with. *I can't tolerate your complaining any longer.*

trans ac tion /tran zak′ shən/ *n.* a business exchange. *The bank clerk entered the day's transactions into the computer records.*

trans con ti nen tal /trans′ kon tə nen′ təl/ *adj.* going across a continent. *The transcontinental railroad was completed in 1869.*

trans fer /trans fûr′/ *v.* **transfers, transferring, transferred.** to move from one place to another. *The new student told us that she had transferred from a private school in California.*

tran si tion /tran zish′ ən/ *n.* a change from one form or stage to another. *The transition from high school to college is sometimes difficult.*

trans late /trans lāt′/ *v.* **translates, translated, translating. 1.** to change into another language. *We are translating poetry in our French class.* **2.** to explain in other words or terms. *Legal terms must sometimes be translated into simpler language.*

trea ty /trē′ tē/ *n., pl.* **treaties.** a formal agreement between nations. *Peace treaties are often signed at the end of wars.*

ty phoon /tī foon′/ *n.* a tropical hurricane. *Typhoons occur in the western part of the Pacific Ocean.*

U

un der dog /un′ dər dôg/ *n.* the one expected to lose. *I often like to cheer for the underdog in a tennis match.*

u ni ty /ū′ ni tē / *n.* the state of being one. *The president tried to bring about national unity in the face of the threat from abroad.*

u ni verse /ū′ nə vûrs′/ *n.* the entire physical world. *The universe includes Earth, all the planets and stars, and everything in space.*

ut most /ut′ mōst/ *adj.* of the greatest or highest degree. *The workers had the utmost respect for the company president.* *n.* the greatest possible; the most. *The players did their utmost to help the team win the game.*

ut ter /ut′ er/ *v.* **utters, uttering, uttered.** to speak aloud. *I uttered a sigh of relief when the knight rescued the damsel in distress.*

V

vac ci nate /vak′ sə nāt′/ *v.* **vaccinates, vaccinating, vaccinated.** to inject a small amount of the dead or weakened germs of a disease into the body so that the body becomes immune. *The doctors vaccinated people against the disease smallpox.*

/a/	at
/ā/	late
/â/	care
/ä/	father
/e/	set
/ē/	me
/i/	it
/ī/	kite
/o/	ox
/ō/	rose
/ô/	brought
	raw
/oi/	coin
/o͝o/	book
/o͞o/	too
/or/	form
/ou/	out
/u/	up
/yo͞o/	cube
/ûr/	turn
	germ
	learn
	firm
	work
/ə/	about
	chicken
	pencil
	cannon
	circus
/ch/	chair
/hw/	which
/ng/	ring
/sh/	shop
/th/	thin
/ᵺ/	there
/zh/	treasure

vague /vāg/ *adj.* not clear. *The vague news report left us wanting to know more.*

valve /valv/ *n.* a device controlling the flow of liquid or gases through a pipe or other container. *The human heart contains valves that control the flow of blood.*

ver ti cal /vûr′ ti kəl/ *adj.* perpendicular to the horizon; straight up and down. *The tall buildings in a big city look vertical from the sidewalks.*

ves sel /ves′ əl/ *n.* a large boat or ship. *Cruise ships are huge vessels.*

vi cious /vish′ əs/ *adj.* **1.** cruel; wicked. *The criminals who had committed the vicious crimes were arrested.* **2.** dangerous or fierce. *The animal control truck came to pick up the vicious dog.*

view point /vū′ point′/ *n.* a way of thinking; mental attitude. *We were very excited to hear her viewpoint.*

vine yard /vin′ yərd/ *n.* an area where grapes are grown. *There are many vineyards in northern California.*

vir tu ous /vûr′ chŏō əs/ *adj.* righteous; good. *Mother Theresa was a woman of virtuous character.*

vol un tar y /vol′ən ter′ ē/ *adj.* performed, done, or made of one's own free will. *It was my voluntary decision to go.*

vul ner a ble /vul′ nər ə bəl/ *adj.* **1.** capable of being hurt, emotionally or physically. *My little sister is very vulnerable to criticism.* **2.** open to danger. *Baby birds in a nest are sometimes vulnerable to other animals.*

W ■■■■■■■■■■■■■■■■

way far er /wā′ fâr′ ər/ *n.* a traveler, especially one who travels on foot. *Minstrels were wayfarers who traveled around Europe in the Middle Ages, playing music and singing songs for a living.*

Y ■■■■■■■■■■■■■■■■

yacht /yot/ *n.* a small ship used for pleasure or racing. *We were looking forward to spending the night on our grandparents' yacht.*

yield /yēld/ *v.* **yields, yielded, yielding. 1.** to give way or to give up. *We yielded to their arguments.* **2.** to produce. *This land will yield a large crop of corn.* **3.** to give control to another. *The defeated troops yielded the town to the enemy.*

A—F Word Bank

G—M Word Bank

_____   _____

_____   _____

_____   _____

_____   _____

_____   _____

_____   _____

_____   _____

_____   _____

_____   _____

_____   _____

_____   _____

_____   _____

_____   _____

_____   _____

_____   _____

_____   _____

_____   _____

_____   _____

N—S Word Bank

T—Z Word Bank

_____   _____

_____   _____

_____   _____

_____   _____

_____   _____

_____   _____

_____   _____

_____   _____

_____   _____

_____   _____

_____   _____

_____   _____

_____   _____

_____   _____

_____   _____

_____   _____

_____   _____

_____   _____

T—Z Word Bank